TELL IT
TO THE FUTURE

TELL IT TO THE FUTURE

*Have I Got A Story For You . . .
about the Twentieth Century*

Francine R. Cefola and Bobbi R. Madry

Golden Quill Press,
a division of Barish-Stern Ltd.

Published By Golden Quill Press
a division of Barish-Stern Ltd.

Copyright © 2018 by Golden Quill Press
ISBN 0-9676256-8-8 Trade
Library of Congress Number 00-104391

All rights reserved, except for appropriate quotes in reviews or scholarly works. Printed in the United States of America. No part of this publication may be reproduced, stored in a retrieval system or transmitted in any form or by any means, electronic, mechanical, photocopying, recording or other without the written permission of the publisher.

New Cover Design Art on Gold Creations - Troutville VA
Original Cover Design by Abacus Graphics, Oceanside, CA
Interior Design by Desktop Miracles, Inc., Stowe, VT
Illustrations by Designs by Donna, New City, NY

ACKNOWLEDGMENTS

Books are produced through the efforts of many people, not just the authors, and this book is no different. *TELL IT TO THE FUTURE—Have I Got A Story For You . . . about the Twentieth Century* would not have been possible without the contributions of the many people who have shared their time, talent and ideas. Our special appreciation goes to the writers who have generously shared their stories and their personal wishes for the future. We thank the following people who served as our independent judges in the *"TELL IT TO THE FUTURE 1998* Writing Contest." Their insight andknowledge helped in the selection of some of the outstanding stories that appear in this book:

Maria Acosta-Jurman, President of M.J. Associates, an event planner, sports marketing and entertainment specialist. She was working on a book about being an entrepreneur.

Anthony M. Cefola, a graduate of Ithaca College, a sports information and computer programmer-specialist who designs websites. He was also the Computer Advisor to The Write Source/Golden Quill Press.

Debby Paine, a story teller, song writer and drama teacher whose first book *There Is Hope*, was published by Golden Quill Press in 1999. Debby owned and operated The Tanning Zone.

Robert Roman, a writer and educator whose articles appeared in the *New York Times, Times Herald Record* and many other newspapers. He was also a candidate for the N.Y. State Assembly.

Barbara Werzansky, a speech pathologist, in private practice specializing in speech therapy and public speaking. She is a published poet and was working on a personal poetry collection.

Our thanks also to Sean Tully, an aspiring writer and intern at Golden Quill Press, who diligently researched the accuracy of dates andevents and made many worth while suggestions.

Proof reading is a difficult task and we are grateful to Kenneth A. Bray of Art on Gold Creations, and Harold E. Winkler for their valuable suggestions.

To Eileen Foti, our deepest appreciation for her generosity and time developing program art.

To Donna Cefola for artistically developing illustrations that enhance the concepts of each decade in *TELL IT TO THE FUTURE.*

To Anthony M. Cefola, who designed our website, then completely re-designed it to market *TELL IT TO THE FUTURE*. We appreciate his talent, abilities, and his dedication.

A special thanks to Dan Madry of Twelve Star Transport for his support and valuable business suggestions.

To our many friends and family members for their support and encouragement.

TABLE OF CONTENTS

Acknowledgments   v
Introduction   xi

CHAPTER 1

1900 – 1909   From Feet and Hooves . . . To Wheels and Wings   1

    Memorable Events of the Decade 2
    Introduction to the Decade and About the Writer 7
    "Love Makes the Difference . . .
        Love the Guiding Force for Families"
        by Mary Bianchini as told to Bobbi R. Madry 8
    Conclusion of the Decade 11

CHAPTER 2

1910 – 1919   Invigorated America Dances to a New Beat   13

    Memorable Events of the Decade 14
    Introduction to the Decade and About the Writer 19
    "Nebraska 1918" by Georgia Strunk 20
    Conclusion of the Decade 24

CHAPTER 3

1920 – 1929   The Roar that Fizzled   25

    Memorable Events of the Decade 27
    Introduction to the Decade and About the Writer 32
    "Street Games" by Lou Baum 33
    Conclusion of the Decade 37

CHAPTER 4

1930 – 1939   And The World Goes Down and Down   39

    Memorable Events of the Decade 40
    Introduction to the Decade and About the Writer 45
    "I Remember Charlie" by Bobbi R. Madry 46
    Conclusion of the Decade 51

CHAPTER 5

1940 – 1949   Marching To War . . . Bonds, Rationing . . .
                A People United   53

    Memorable Events of the Decade 54
    Introduction to the Decade and About the Writer 59
    "A Look to the Past" by Eileen M. Foti 60
    Introduction to the Story and About the Writer 64
    "Recalling a Father and D-day 1944"
        by Jean M. Olwell 64
    Conclusion of the Decade 67

CHAPTER 6

1950 – 1959   Fast Forwarding into the Fabulous Fifties . . .
                the Best of Times   69

    Memorable Events of the Decade 70
    Introduction to the Decade and About the Writer 75
    "The Magic Box" by Fran Toepfer 76
    Introduction to the Story and About the Writer 78
    "Off to the Bungalow" by Francine R. Cefola 78
    Introduction to the Story and About the Writers 83
    "That's How It Should Be"
        by Marilyn Benkler and Ellen Ziegler 84
    Conclusion of the Decade 87

Table of Contents   ix

CHAPTER 7

1960 – 1969   A Time Of Love . . . A Time Of Hate . . .
               A Nation Rocked By Change   89

    Memorable Events of the Decade 90
    Introduction to the Decade and About the Writer 95
    "Impressions—from the Sixties" by Anne M. Ogle 96
    Introduction to the Story and About the Writer 98
    "Reflections: On Where Have All the
       Flowers Gone?" by Robert Reeg 98
    Introduction to the Story and About the Writer 102
    "Reflections on the Assassination of
       Dr. Martin Luther King, Jr." by Naomi G. Anthony . .102
    Conclusion of the Decade 107

CHAPTER 8

1970 – 1979   From Crisis To Calm and Back Again . . .
               Where Do We Go From Here?   109

    Memorable Events of the Decade 110
    Introduction to the Decade and About the Writer 116
    "On America's Golden Road" by Theresa Zarrella 117
    Conclusion of the Decade 121

CHAPTER 9

1980 – 1989   A Click of the Mouse . . . a Zoom into Space . . .
               Stock Market Up . . . Stock Market Down   123

    Memorable Events of the Decade 124
    Introduction to the Decade and About the Writer 129
    "My Children's Gift of Courage" by Beth Rubin 130
    Conclusion of the Decade 135

CHAPTER 10

1990 – 1999 A Time For Looking Back . . .
A Time For Looking Forward 137

    Memorable Events of the Decade 138
    Introduction to the Decade 143
    "Remembering Desert Storm" by Francine R. Cefola
        and Bobbi R. Madry 144
    Introduction to the Story and About the Writer 145
    "Chasing the Dream . . . The Life of a Yankee Fan"
        by Carianne Carleo-Evangelist 145
    Introduction to the Story and About the Writer 151
    "The Y2K Nightmare" by Anthony M. Cefola 152
    Conclusion of the Decade 157

CHAPTER 11

2000 – The Twenty First Century and Beyond . . .
What Will the Future Bring? 159

    Introduction to the New Century 160
    "Music Through the Century"
        by Francine R. Cefola and Bobbi R. Madry 164
    Moving Into the Next Century .164
    "Hopes and Wishes for the Future" by the Authors
        and Writers 165
    What Will Our Legacy Be? 169

Authors' Biographies 170

INTRODUCTION

Storytelling has played an enormous role in our ability to communicate our thoughts and feelings about the past and our hopes and dreams for the future. Before spoken and written languages, printing presses and present day technologies, stories were passed down, from generation to generation, informing and educating us while providing our major source of entertainment.

As the authors of *TELL IT TO THE FUTURE—Have I Got A Story For You . . . about the Twentieth Century*, we went into our communities and listened to stories from people of all generations. We realized that unless their stories were written down they would vanish and be treasures lost, never to be regained. We found that many young people had very little knowledge of the beginning of our century and of the time before they were born. They often felt history was boring, but enjoyed hearing stories they could relate to the lives their parents or grandparents experienced, and were fascinated to learn about the world before computers, television, cars and planes.

As authors of *TELL IT TO THE FUTURE,* we have endeavored to create a time capsule of printed pages and beautiful illustrations that paint memorable pictures of the twentieth century. When we look back through the pages of time, history is filled with major events that have affected and often changed the world . . . sometimes for better, sometimes for worse. To list every category and event and to pay tribute to all the deserving people of the times, would take volumes. Instead, we have focused on each decade of the twentieth century listing important dates and giving a sketch of events that affected and influenced our country—the United States of America. We have included information we feel gives the reader a visual sense of the times.

This book is designed to give you, the reader, enjoyment and information, whether you read it chapter by chapter, by favorite decades, or by one story or timeline at a time. Each chapter contains a timeline that lists Major Events of the United States and World History, Important Advances in Science and Technology, Spotlight on the World of Entertainment, Sports' Highlights and Other Interesting Facts.

You will be transported into each decade through a time portal that places you there and lets you experience that time. Even if you have no idea how it would feel to be an immigrant coming to this country, or what it was like to be a young child living in a tenement without modern conveniences, these stories will take you there. You'll cross the prairie in a schooner, fall in love in the thirties, visit a farm and go to war. You'll relive the changes and challenges of the fifties, and the onset of television, feel the turbulence of the sixties, and walk through civil rights with Dr. King. You'll travel America's Golden Road and deal with AIDS, pray through Desert Storm, cheer on the Yankees and hold your breath as we approach Y2K. You will come full circle as we count down the century and experience the best and worst of the old, welcome the new, and share the hopes and dreams of all our writers.

There were so many events that impacted on our country, we wish we could have found stories for all of them. We are therefore taking this opportunity to salute all the dedicated men and women who served our country, to protect out shores and help ensure our freedom. We also pay tribute to all Americans, past and present, who contributed to making our country great.

TELL IT TO THE FUTURE—Have I Got A Story For You . . . about the Twentieth Century, was written by writers of diverse backgrounds, from all over the United States, with ages ranging from early twenties to late nineties. It is the hope of all our writers that their experiences will be of benefit to all generations in uniting us as one world to help our children take us proudly into the future. It is by understanding where we came from . . . how we got here and where our combined efforts can take us, that we will achieve our goals of creating a world that offers a bright and promising future for all.

DEDICATION

*"There are only two powers in the world, the sword and the pen;
And in the end the former is always conquered by the latter."*

NAPOLEON

*With hopes for the future we dedicate this book
to all writers and storytellers, who have a burning desire
to touch others with their words.
We also dedicate this book to all our readers.
May you find each story entertaining and informative
while giving you pause for thought.*

1900's

1

From Feet and Hooves . . .
To Wheels and Wings

1900-1909

*This was a brand new century;
it was a time of adventure,
exploration and change.*

Memorable Events of the Decade

PRESIDENTS AND THEIR FIRST LADIES

1901	25th	William McKinley	First Lady Ida Saxton
1901–1909	26th	Theodore Roosevelt	First Lady Edith Kermit Carow
1909	27th	William H. Taft	First Lady Helen Herron

MAJOR EVENTS OF THE UNITED STATES AND WORLD HISTORY

1900 The Open Door Policy establishes multi-nation trade with China on an equal basis

Hawaii becomes a territory of the United States

Germany's Second Fleet Act establishes a plan to double the size of their navy within 20 years

The Boxer Rebellion heightens when the Empress orders all foreigners in China killed

1901 President McKinley is assassinated by anarchist Leon Czolgosz

Vice President Roosevelt, at 42 becomes the youngest man ever to become President

J.P. Morgan buys Carnegie Steel and 10 other companies to create the U.S. Steel Corporation

1904 Work begins on the Panama Canal, which would shorten world trade routes

The Japanese start the Russo-Japanese War with a surprise attack on a Russian Naval Base

1905 Tzar Nicholas II gives orders to shoot unarmed factory workers marching to present grievances

1906 San Francisco earthquake destroys most of the city and leaves a half million people homeless

President Roosevelt wins the Nobel Peace Prize for helping end the Russo-Japanese War

1907 U.S. prohibits Japanese from entering America

SunYat-Sen establishes the Democratic Republic of China

Panic on Wall Street causes a run on banks, is stopped by J.P. Morgan's 100 million in gold

From Feet and Hooves . . . To Wheels and Wings 3

1909 Robert Peary achieves his goal of reaching the North Pole, called "the roof of the world"

IMPORTANT ADVANCES IN SCIENCE AND TECHNOLOGY

1900 Max Planck formulates his quantum theory that energy is not absorbed or radiated continuously

Benjamin Holt invents the farm tractor

Sigmund Freud writes *The Interpretation of Dreams*, delving into the unconscious mind

George Eastman introduces the Brownie, the first affordable mass-market camera

1901 The first transatlantic radio transmission is achieved

Gillette introduces the safety razor for shaving

1902 Carrier develops air conditioning as a way to cool large areas

1903 Wright brothers, Orville and Wilbur, fly the first powered plane at Kitty Hawk, North Carolina

1904 Henry Ford organizes the Ford Motor Company to produce automobiles

New York City subway, an underground train system, opens

Mary Mallon, a Long Island cook, nicknamed "Typhoid Mary," spreads the disease

1905 Einstein conceives the theory of relativity, $e=mc^2$ that time is relative

1906 Alva Fisher invents the washing machine for cleaning clothes

1908 First upright vacuum, an electrical suction sweeper, is invented by J. Murray Spangler

Ford Motor Company produces the first "Model T"—price, $850, in one color, black

Hans Geiger invents the Geiger Counter, a device that measures radioactivity

1909 Synthetic plastics, materials capable of being molded or shaped, are developed

Dr. Paul Ehrlich discovers a cure for syphilis

SPOTLIGHT ON THE WORLD OF ENTERTAINMENT

1900 Scott Joplin's Ragtime music becomes popular

Popular artists: Picasso, Gauguin, Cezanne, Renoir, and Toulouse-Lautrec

Magician Harry Houdini, escapes from shackles, straitjackets and locked trunks

L. Frank Baum's *The Wonderful Wizard of Oz,* takes readers over the rainbow

1901 Roosevelt invites black author, Booker T. Washington, to dinner at the White House

The Settlement Cookbook is published by social worker Lizzie Black

1902 Opera star, Enrico Caruso makes his first record, sound in a spiral groove on a disk or cylinder

1903 *The Great Train Robbery*, the longest film, runs 12 minutes

Jack London writes *Call of the Wild*, his experiences in Alaska during the Gold Rush '97-'98

Barbershop quartets had men harmonizing *Sweet Adeline* together while waiting for the barber

1904 James Barrie's theme of a boy who doesn't want to grow up is portrayed in *Peter Pan*

1905 The first Nickelodeon theatre, showing short silent films for 5 cents opens in Pittsburgh

1906 "Muckrakers," journalists who expose corruption and dishonesty become influential

Upton Sinclair's *The Jungle* brings about the U.S. Pure Food and Drug Act

Ruth St. Denis introduces modern dance

Ferdinand "Jelly Roll" Morton becomes a star with his ragtime hit *King Porter Stomp*

1907 Ziegfeld presents the Follies; stage extravaganzas features beautiful women and elaborate costumes

Pablo Picasso establishes Cubism, an abstract style of art which separates subjects into cubes

First daily comic strip *Mr. Mutt,* by Bud Fisher begins

From Feet and Hooves . . . To Wheels and Wings

SPORTS' HIGHLIGHTS

1900 First Davis Cup, U.S. beats Britain in this International tennis tournament

Baseball cards are given free with cigarettes

Dribbling, bouncing the ball to keep it in motion or move forward, becomes a part of basketball

Ice Hockey officially begins with a face-off to decide first possession of the hockey puck

William Muldoon named first professional wrestling champion

1903 Baseball's Boston Red Sox defeat the Pittsburgh Pirates in the first modern World Series

1904 Baseball's Cy Young pitches a perfect game, no opposing player gets on base

1905 60 major colleges form the Intercollegiate Athletic Association

1906 U.S. Lawn Tennis—Winners: Men's – William Clothier; Women's – Helen Homans

1908 Jack Johnson knocks out Tommy Burns to become the first black heavyweight champ

Chicago's "Tinker to Evers to Chance," baseball's best known double play combination

1909 The Indianapolis 500 race track is completed

OTHER INTERESTING FACTS

1900 Average American salary 22 cents per hour

45 States—approximately 76 million people

Only four states, all in the west, permit woman to vote

John Luther "Casey" Jones sacrifices himself to save the passengers of the Cannonball Express

The International Ladies' Garment Workers Union forms—goals improve sweatshop conditions

1901 Instant coffee, which can be made by the cup, is introduced

Nabisco introduces **BARNUM'S ANIMAL CRACKERS**, cookies shaped like different animals

American cheese, processed cheddar cheese, is created by James Kraft

Ludwig Roselius invents 97% caffeine-free coffee

1902 CRAYOLA CRAYONS, multicolored wax markers, are introduced by Binney and Smith

TEDDY BEARS get their name from a cartoon about Teddy Roosevelt refusing to shoot a bear cub

1904 Russo-Japanese War sees the first use of trenches, ditches dug for cover and concealment

St. Louis World's Fair, features exhibitions from many countries and the first American Olympics

Woman is arrested in New York for smoking a cigarette in public

When an ice cream stand runs out of plates they use rolled waffles—the first ice cream cones

1905 Helen Keller, blind, deaf and dumb from birth, graduates from prestigious, Radcliffe College

Mary Anderson invents windshield wipers

First Rotary Club, organization of business and professional people is founded in Chicago

1906 President T. Roosevelt is the first U.S. president to travel outside the United States

15 states put 20 miles per hours into effect as a speed limit

1907 First Sunday in May is established in Philadelphia as Mothers' Day

The first paper towel is introduced by the Scott Paper Co.

Ovorono, the first underarm deodorant, is marketed for women only

First time a ball is dropped in Times Square to signify the New Year

1908 Irons, heated metal for smoothing wrinkled clothes and toasters for browning bread are introduced

1909 America steps into the age of radio with regular broadcasting

George Hellman begins marketing mayonnaise based on his wife's recipe

INTRODUCTION TO THE DECADE

The turn of the century signified a time of optimism and hope as the United States moved forward with new ideas and inventions. We were growing and prospering as we progressed to motor powered vehicles and like birds, man had found his wings.

The promise of a better life brought millions of immigrants to our shores. Mary's Bianchini and her family were among the many immigrants who, in the 1900's, were greeted by the sight of the Statue of Liberty and processed through Ellis Island before beginning their new lives in the United States.

Mary's family settled in Rockland County, thirty miles north of Manhattan, where she grew up to be one of the county's most honored citizens. As a nurse, radio and television personality and community activist, she championed a number of causes which led her to being honored by four United States Presidents.

At the age of ninety, Mary met author, editor Bobbi Madry and the two collaborated to produce Mary's story, "Love Makes The Difference—Reflections on life in Rockland County." Bobbi, who was the Educational Director for The Write Source and Golden Quill Press, masterfully captured Mary's philosophy of life; her ideas on building family values and the reasons why every citizen should be involved in community growth. In celebration of the book and for her ninety-second birthday, in 1999, The Write Source and Golden Quill Press held a fund raiser to support the Mary Costino Bianchini Scholarship Fund, which they established at Rockland Community College. At that event, Congressman Benjamin Gilman, of New York, read a proclamation that was introduced into the Congressional Record saluting Mary's many accomplishments. This story is taken from Mary's life, as told to and written by Bobbi Madry.

Love Makes the Difference...
Love the Guiding Force
for Families

Mary Bianchini as told to Bobbi R. Madry

Every time I hear the National Anthem, I give thanks that my parents immigrated to America and that I am an American citizen. Immigrants have been and are still bringing their varied customs and cultures to America and contributing to the rich tapestry of our nation. Before coming to America, my parents, Valentine and Theresa Costino lived in Malfalda, Italy, which is south of Rome. After the turn of the century, my father, (we called him Poppa), a shoemaker by trade, decided to come to America to build a new life for his family. He wanted to establish his niche in his new homeland, then send for my mother, and my brother Nicholas, who was just two years old. Mother was three months pregnant with me.

Father embarked on his journey with great excitement. He wasn't worried about establishing himself because he had friends already in the United States who would help him learn the ropes. He knew he would need to improve his English to be able to communicate effectively.

Before father could arrange to bring his family to America, an epidemic of typhoid spread throughout our village and my beloved little brother Nicholas died. Mother was distraught and fearful that when I was born I would be affected too. When mother gave birth to me in March 1907, I was somewhat sickly, but typhoid free. It must have been the goat's milk that pulled me through, but they also used leeches behind my ears to draw out the blood to hasten healing and help my body fight any other diseases. The irony of this was that at that time the leeches were being imported to Europe from a druggist in Nyack, New York, where my family later settled.

During this ordeal father wasn't able to come back to Italy because he needed to work. In the early 1900's there wasn't airplane service from one country to another. Also, you couldn't just pick up a telephone and call anyplace in the world, so mother and father had to keep in contact by mail that went to and from countries by ship.

It wasn't until I was past the age of two that Poppa was able to send for his family. Although he was a fine shoemaker by trade, he had not been able to find work except as a stone crusher at Rockland Lake, which is thirty miles north of New York City. Father had lived in a boarding house until he could provide a place to live, then bring his family to America.

Upon our arrival at Ellis Island, we were examined and processed before we were allowed to officially enter the United States. My mother had all our papers in proper order so we were not classified "WOPS," which meant "without passports." The word "WOP" is a slang term, but is sometimes used to insult others, generally, by people who don't know this is what it means.

Poppa was supposed to meet us, but we learned that he had gotten lost. Mother spoke no English but was not one to sit and wait for long. When Poppa didn't show up and she could find no means of transportation, she set out on foot with me in one hand and a suitcase in the other. This was a time before super highways and highspeed cars, actually before any cars if you can imagine that. People still relied on horses, boats or trains or their feet. I don't know how Mother expected to cross the Hudson River, but Poppa figured she'd be trudging northward and somehow, with the help of friendly people, they found one another and the family was reunited.

"Paesanos," as Italians were called, helped one another find work and Rockland Lake was where my father found work cutting, storing and moving ice. At that time people had ice boxes, not refrigerators, so a lot of ice came from Rockland Lake.

Being an ambitious man, my father soon opened a shoe repair shop and a general store to provide families in the area with supplies such as groceries, pots and pans and other household needs. My mother was a genius at keeping records and doing the arithmetic required. She picked up the language and what she couldn't communicate in words, she managed to convey with a smile and an understanding heart.

In those days we had no prepared frozen foods. You cooked your meals from scratch every day. When it came to getting laundry done you relied on the old wash board, bar soap, a kettle in which to heat water over a wood stove and a wash and rinse tub. If you didn't have a hand operated wringer, you twisted each garment or item by hand to squeeze out the soapy water, then again after rinsing. From there each piece was shaken out and pinned to a line with wooden clothes pins.

We managed to serve our customers quite well. We had rows of well built shelves stacked with dry goods (cloth to sew) and numerous household items such as brooms, mops, buckets, dishes, cookware and school supplies. Shelves were stacked to the ceiling with canned and dried goods and packaged foods. There were barrels, baskets, sacks and wooden boxes containing bulk foods. You were helped to get your grocery order together, then if necessary, it was weighed then tallied by hand. A part of the service in the old time general store of the early 1900's was a friendly smile of welcome when you came in and "Thank you, come back soon," when you left.

My early childhood years were spent in a closely knit family that followed the traditions of love of God, family, country, neighbor and being a moral and caring individual. Our parents were strict, but disciplined us with love. They knew we had to learn to grow up to be responsible adults who could take their place in society as respected members of the community. These early lessons have been my guidelines throughout life.

In recent years, I had an opportunity to visit Ellis Island, now restored and the Statue of Liberty and I felt a surge of pride in being an American citizen. I think every citizen, whether immigrant or native born, should stop occasionally and give thanks for the blessings of this great country.

Conclusion of the Decade

At the conclusion of this decade, Americans were looking forward to accelerated progress and prosperity. Women were beginning to take a stand for their rights and issues of the abuse of child labor spawned a need for social reform. As we closed the page of this first decade, the focus would become rapid communication and transportation. The popular waltzes of the early 1900's gave way to Ragtime and Dixieland Jazz, and the faster pace of life propelled us into the second decade. Amidst the possibilities for growth was an increasing unrest in the world which would have a significant impact on our lives.

1910's

2

Invigorated America Dances to a New Beat

1910-1919

Then the nation mobilizes for the fight . . .
war and prohibition.

Memorable Events of the Decade

PRESIDENTS AND THEIR FIRST LADIES

1910–1913 27th William H. Taft   First Lady Helen Herron
1913–1919 28th Woodrow Wilson   First Lady Ellen Axson, Edith Galt

MAJOR EVENTS OF THE UNITED STATES AND WORLD HISTORY

1910 Japan builds its military might in Asia after the Russo-Japanese War and annexes Korea

1911 Standard Oil Company having a monopoly violates the Sherman Antitrust Act, and is broken up

1912 The "unsinkable" Titanic, sinks on her maiden voyage, killing over 1,500 people

War in the Balkans, sets the stage for World War I

1913 Income Tax is made legal with the passage of the Sixteenth Amendment

5,000 women demanding the right to vote, called Suffragists, are attacked by male bystanders

1914 Assassination of Archduke Ferdinand of Austria triggers the start of World War I

Panama Canal opens linking the Atlantic and Pacific Oceans

1915 German U-boat sinks the "Lusitania" killing 1,198 passengers

William J. Simmons revives the Ku Klux Klan, a sect advocating white supremacy

1916 Communists overthrow Russia's Czar Nicholas Romanov

Jeanette Rankin of Montana becomes the first women to be elected to Congress

1917 U.S. enters World War I

1918 The war is over—Germany and her allies are defeated

1919 Treaty of Versailles is signed—terms lead Germany to economic collapse and World War II

Communism, the theory of government ownership in a classless society, was spreading

Invigorated America Dances to a New Beat

Prohibition ends legal alcohol consumption—organized crime profits from illegal sales

IMPORTANT ADVANCES IN SCIENCE AND TECHNOLOGY

1910 Halley's comet is seen

1910 Georges Claude invents neon lighting

1911 Charles Kettering develops an electric starter for cars

Roald Amundsen, a Norwegian explorer, becomes the first person to reach the South Pole

Casimir Funk discovers thiamine and coins the term, "vital amines" shortened to "vitamin"

1912 Stainless Steel is invented

The Piltdown Man, the "missing link" of man and ape is discovered—later found to be a hoax

Gideon Sundback invents the zipper

1913 Henry Ford uses the assembly line to speed production of the Model-T

The 55 story Woolworth Building in New York City, the tallest building in the world is completed

1914 Mary P. Jacob designs the first women's brassiere

1915 Albert Einstein unveils his "Theory of Relativity"

1916 Mechanical home refrigerators are introduced

1917 Sigmund Freud introduces psychoanalysis

1918 Four million American workers strike for better working conditions and wages

Frederick Banting and Charles Best discover Insulin

Electric mixer is invented by Universal Company

1918 Rorschach tests, or "Ink-blots" are introduced by psychiatrist Hermann Rorschach

SPOTLIGHT ON THE WORLD OF ENTERTAINMENT

1910 Ballerina Anna Pavlova dances at the Met in New York City

1911 Leonardo da Vinci's, *Mona Lisa* is stolen from the Louvre art museum in Paris

Irving Berlin debuts the new musical style with *Alexander's Ragtime Band*

1911 Joseph Pulitzer wills money to establish the Pulitzer Prize awards

1912 Mack Sennett produces silent film slapstick comedy—*Keystone Kops* film series

Basis for the Montessori schools is explained in the best-seller, *The Montessori Method*

1913 The Armory Show in New York introduces European artists, such as Picasso and Matisse

Missing for 2 years the *Mona Lisa* is recovered in Italy

The *Tango* becomes a dance craze, and is banned in Boston

Stravinsky's *The Rite of Spring* shocks audiences with its wild style, changing classical music

1914 *St. Louis Blues* by W.C. Handy epitomizes Southern blues

Edgar Rice Burrough's *Tarzan of the Apes,* tells the tale of a baby raised by apes in the jungle

1915 D.W. Griffith's controversial *Birth of a Nation* is the most successful and expensive film ever

Silent film star Charlie Chaplin's "The Tramp" with bowler hat, cane and baggy clothes wins fans

1916 Norman Rockwell's illustrations of small town life first appears in the Saturday Evening Post

Dixieland Jazz Band cuts the first jazz record

1917 George M. Cohan writes the patriotic theme *Over There*

Russian exile, 16-year-old violinist, Jascha Heifetz, makes his U.S. debut at Carnegie Hall

1919 Vaudeville, musical comedy and variety acts are appearing in over 900 theatres

Chicago becomes the capital for Jazz

SPORTS' HIGHLIGHTS

1910 Jack Johnson defeats Jeff Jeffries retaining his heavyweight title

President Taft throws out the first ball of the baseball season—starting that tradition

Invigorated America Dances to a New Beat

1911 U.S. Open golf tournament first American champion Johnny McDermott

Pitching legend Cy Young retires

Golfer Bobby Jones wins his first title, the Junior Championship of Atlanta at age 9

1912 American Indian Jim Thorpe wins the pentathlon and decathlon at the Stockholm Olympics

1913 Amateur golfer Francis Ouimet defeats England's pros

1915 Georgia Tech defeats Cumberland College 222-0, in a football game

1916 Bobby Jones' popularity takes golf from the elite into the world of the masses

1917 New York's Polo Grounds host the first Sunday baseball game breaking the blue laws

1919 *Sir Barton,* ridden by Johnny Loftus, becomes the 1st horse to win the Triple Crown

Baseball's Chicago White Sox team throw the 1919 World Series in the "Black Sox Scandal"

OTHER INTERESTING FACTS

1910 MANN ACT made it illegal to take a women across state lines for immoral purposes

146 Triangle Shirtwaist factory workers are killed by fire when the owners trap them inside

OREO cookies, chocolate wafers with vanilla cream inside are introduced

LIFESAVERS, fruit flavored hard candy with a hole in the center are introduced

The F.W. Woolworth Company becomes the world's largest retail chain with 596 stores

1913 Erector sets, that let children build objects, become popular

Crossword puzzles are the brain child of Arthur Wynne

Coco Chanel revolutionizes women's fashion with practical and fashionable clothes

Striking garment workers get pay raises and shorter hours

1914 The RAGGEDY ANN doll is invented by a terminally ill girl's mother

1915 Margaret Sanger opens the first birth control clinic, to help prevent unwanted pregnancies

1916 Daylight Savings Time is introduced to save fuel, but is repealed when farmers complain

OVOMALTINE, egg, malt, milk and cocoa is introduced in America as OVALTINE

QUAKER OATS introduces the first "instant" oatmeal you can make in a bowl without cooking

1918 First home use of refrigerators, to keep food cold is introduced

20 million killed by worldwide flu epidemic—500,000 of them Americans

Lt. George Boyle makes the first airmail flight—stamps cost 24 cents, 3 cents for regular mail

Robert LeRoy Ripley begins his *Believe it or Not!* series

Food administrator, Herbert Hoover implements food rationing for the war effort

Invigorated America Dances to a New Beat

INTRODUCTION TO THE DECADE

Progress was the key word at the beginning of the second decade of the century. Manufacturing was America's leading industry and it established the differences between the working class, "the blue collar workers" and the bosses, "the white collar class." Many immigrants were pouring into America to escape the war in Europe and were finding jobs in the automobile and railroad industries. But as the war in Europe waged on, it became obvious that the United States was headed for war and in 1917 we entered the fighting. Men and materials supplied by the United States helped end the war by 1918, but the soldiers came home to the beat of a different American drum. Women were fighting for their rights, workers were striking for better conditions and the end of legal alcohol consumption led to a rise in organized crime.

Although there was enormous progress, many people living on farms and in small villages still lived simple lives. Georgia Strunk and her family lived in Nebraska during the 1910's where "recycling" was an everyday practice. The family made sure to re-use whatever was possible and enjoyed spending quality time together. As a child, Georgia remembers that the war seemed far away, but there were everyday reminders in the shortages of items like coal and paper. Georgia Strunk today looks back on the second decade of the century with fond memories and asks the question, "Were we worse off for having fewer conveniences?" She doesn't think so. In 1999 Georgia Strunk, was in her eighties, but still enjoyed sharing her stories about how living in Nebraska in 1918, prepared her for life and how she was able to overcome the hardships of life in primitive Alaska thirty years later. Now, we the reader, can glimpse into what life was like, in "Nebraska 1918."

Nebraska 1918

Georgia Strunk

During my childhood, I grew up in Nebraska where life was very different. There were no radio or television programs, videos or movies. There were only a few telephones and of course those were the famous party lines—a source of much shared information, whether you cared to hear it or not.

Since then the telegraph and telephone, radio, television and the computer have all changed the way we communicate around the world. I remember the telegraph lines were all along the railroad tracks and a system of morse code, a sequence of dots and dashes that translate into words, was used. Then came the telephone, and the ability to speak and hear the voice of the other person. In each village in Nebraska, there was a central office with an operator. When you wanted to make a call you would turn the crank on the phone and be connected to the operator who would respond by asking for the party you wanted to reach. Party lines which have all the phone lines of an area on one line were wonderful for communication with your neighbors, but awful when you wanted privacy. When you received a call the phone would ring in a certain pattern: number of rings, short or long, signaling that the call was for a specific person.

For entertainment we had the exciting traveling circus called, "Buffalo Bill's." The circus was conducted by the famous Wild Bill Cody, whose hometown was North Platte, Nebraska. A popular show in the circus was the trained pig act where little piglets were dressed in the styles of the day and were pushed around in doll carriages.

When we weren't at the circus, we were at home helping, or going to school. I started school in 1918. I wore high top shoes that had rows of tiny buckles. My dresses had many petticoats underneath the skirts to make them stand out. Jeans and slacks were unheard of for girls. There were no permanent hair waves back then and most girls wore their hair long and in braids.

Education in Nebraska, in 1918 consisted of a one room schoolhouse with one teacher, coal oil lamps for light, coal burning stoves for heat and hand-pumped water. The day started at 9:00 A.M. and dismissed at 4:00 P.M. Four students to a seat listened to prayers from the bible, the pledge of allegiance, songs and a chapter from a book by a current author. Great minds developed from that one-room school house.

In school and at home, we learned to use everything. Recycling used items is not a new practice. Back then, in front of every store was a huge barrel used to collect cans, used jar lids, gum wrappers and paper sacks. At home we kept the paper sacks to write and color on. We never wasted a piece of paper, or anything else. One day as I was coming home from school, a lady was depositing paper sacks in the barrel and I asked if I might have her sacks. She said they were to go for the war effort. I didn't fully understand what the war was about, so I explained to her that I wanted to become an artist, but didn't have anything to write or draw on. So the lady gave me the sacks.

The next day, the same lady was at the barrel again and this time she gave me more paper and a new box of crayons and pencils. I was so thrilled. I don't ever remember having a whole box of crayons before that I didn't have to divide with my sister.

Catalogs were a main source of shopping. My sister Eloyce and I played paper dolls with figures we cut from the Sears and Roebuck catalogs. We got the colored pages, but the rest was delegated to become toilet paper. That was a time well before we had many of today's paper products.

A standard part of homes in Nebraska was the storm cellar because the state was plagued with cyclones and tornados. Our cellar had a rounded dome over an area dug six to eight feet below ground. The storm cellars of that decade had multiple uses and were commonly known as "caves." A good, sturdy wooden door was hung at the bottom of the dirt steps, with a slanted double door, up on ground level for quick access. Our cellar also served as a reprieve from stifling hot summers and a cool place to store canned and preserved produce for the winter months. We kept our milk, butter, cheese and garden vegetables and fruits there.

I remember one day when a dark funnel cloud sent everyone scurrying for the "cave." My father grabbed the tin box he kept all our important papers in, such as insurance, marriage license and small valuables, and hurried my mother, who was carrying baby Helen, down the storm cellar steps. Then he grabbed Eloyce and me and dove for cover. Just as he closed the bottom door, the wind blew off the outside doors and also ripped out the six inch square vent that let in light and air through the cellar roof. We huddled together in the dark trembling to the roar of the cyclone. When all was quiet again, my father opened the door and we crawled up the steps. The place where the barn had been was swept clean. Chickens were running in the yard minus their feathers and some of those poor chickens ended up in the stew pot.

Our neighbors were less fortunate . . . they lost their home. Someone said, "Well, they didn't have much anyway," but my mother answered, "it was all they had . . . anyway." Another of our neighbors was a German man who had been in the United States before World War I started. He admired my mother's white leghorn chickens because they were excellent laying hens. He would "slip" some of our chickens into his hen house. He probably thought we couldn't prove whose white chickens were whose. My mother solved that by dipping her chickens in the dark blueing solution she used for washing clothes. People thought the eggs from blue chickens would be blue and that brought a great demand for our eggs, but it didn't work that way. It did, however, keep our stock from "wandering" off to our neighbors hen house.

During the time our nation was at war, food was scarce and coal was at a premium. We girls would pull our wagon along the railroad tracks seeking spilled coal chunks. Some of the firemen on the trains would manage to lose a little extra coal along our stretch of the track. Then the Armistice was signed in November 1918.

About that time, due to my fathers failing health, he sold the threshing machine and horses he had used in his business traveling throughout Kansas and Nebraska. We then moved to Wilsonville,

Nebraska to a small area known as Skunk Hollow. We traveled by wagon, which was then known as a prairie schooner. My mother walked part of the time beside the horses, but being too young to walk with her, my sister and I had to amuse ourselves in the wagon. One evening we pulled to a stop to allow a train to pass. I had been hanging over the front of the wagon and the sudden stop jolt, threw me out. My father said he searched frantically for me in the dark and finally found me clinging to the wagon tongue, right under the skittery horses. I was under my mother's eye the rest of the trip.

Yes, life was very different during my childhood. Saturday night was bath time. The water was drawn by hand pump and put in the copper boiler to heat on top of the wood stove. We used soap our Mother made. She always added vanilla or lemon scent to give it fragrance. The washtub bathing ritual, which was held behind the kitchen stove, ran from the youngest child to the oldest. We had to place chairs around the tub for privacy. Following the bath, we put on our fresh clean underwear and nightgowns. One night as I was getting out of the tub, I bent over too far and made contact with the front door of the kitchen stove, which bore the insignia of the Rose Manufacturing Company, a "hot" rose. Friends at school wondered why I didn't sit down for weeks.

As I look back over that decade, I wonder if I am any worse for wear for having ridden in a covered wagon, pumped water, hoed gardens, bathed in wash tubs, ate off tin plates, drank from tin cups, drank unsterilized milk, wore clothes my mother made, went to school in a one room schoolhouse, walked to outside toilets and played basketball in big, baggy, black bloomers. Am I worse for having chopped wood and studied by a coal oil lamp? I don't think so. For all of the "backwoods ways," we also went to church regularly and were taught great respect for our parents, for ourselves and for others.

I will be the first one to say I like all of the modern conveniences like radios, television, refrigerators, cell phones and indoor plumbing. Yes, this is also a great decade. But I remember Nebraska in 1918 and my childhood. It was a great age, an age of simplicity and family togetherness, that will never be again.

Conclusion of the Decade

By the conclusion of the decade and the end of World War I, Americans could once again look forward to technological progress being directed toward domestic use. Although the economic picture was slowly improving, families across the nation still lacked many modern conveniences. And although Henry Ford's plant was producing cars by the thousands, the horse was still being relied upon for transportation. The fledgling film industry was thriving and motion pictures soon replaced the popular nickelodeon that once cranked flip cards to allow you to see a series of actions, like dancing girls. Movies were influencing daily life and the tailored, modest and understated dress of this decade would give way to the free and flashy dress of the twenties. America's pace would change drastically, accelerated by rapid communications and transportation. As we roared into the twenties, the major changes in daily life such as those caused by prohibition and organized crime, would bring about the most unexpected events.

We dedicate this chapter to all the men and women who served our country during World War I to protect our shores and safeguard our country's freedom.

3

The Roar that Fizzled

1920-1929

*Prosperity bubbled like champagne
bringing fast times, speakeasies
and organized crime. . . .
then it all came crashing down.*

1920's

The Roar that Fizzled

Memorable Events of the Decade

PRESIDENTS AND THEIR FIRST LADIES

1921–1923 29th Warren G. Harding   First Lady Florence DeWolfe
1923–1929 30th Calvin Coolidge   First Lady Grace Goodhue
1929   31st Herbert Hoover   First Lady Lou Henry

MAJOR EVENTS OF THE UNITED STATES AND WORLD HISTORY

1920 The 19th amendment gives women the right to vote

Mohandas Gandhi leads a nonviolent reform movement in India

U.S. Attorney General orders raids on list of "moral perverts and misguided anarchists"

League of Women Voters is founded in New York State, to keep women voters informed

Social reformers create the American Civil Liberties Union to protect our rights

1921 The Emergency Quota Act is the first time limitations are established for immigrants

1922 Interior Secretary Fall grants the Teapot Dome's oil reserves to Mammoth Oil, for gifts and loans

Calling himself, "Il Duce," the leader, Italy's Benito Mussolini established a fascist state

1923 Ku Klux Klan activities spur Oklahoma Governor Walton to declare martial law

President Mustafa Kemal reforms Turkey separating government from religious control

1924 Joseph Stalin becomes leader of the Communist Party and begins his purge of the Soviet Union

The Johnson-Reed Act further restricts immigration

1925 "Monkey trial" convicts John T. Scopes for teaching evolution in Tennessee schools

1926 Emperor Hirohito builds Japan's military strength and fosters aggression toward foreign nations

1927 Chiang Kai-shek captures Shanghai and Nanjing to unite China under one government

1928 Richard E. Byrd begins an expedition to the Antarctic

1929 "Black Tuesday," October 29, stock market collapse, start of the depression

Arabs in Palestine make their first major attack on Jews

IMPORTANT ADVANCES IN SCIENCE AND TECHNOLOGY

1920 Surgeon Harvey Cushing develops new techniques in brain surgery

Westinghouse introduces the first mass-market radios

1924 Edwin Hubble calculates the Andromeda galaxy is one million light years away

1925 Clarence Birdseye perfects the process for freezing food

1926 Physicist Robert Goddard uses liquid-fuel for rocket launch

1927 Georges Lemaitre's *Big Bang Theory,* the universe began with a massive explosion

The first underwater automobile tunnel, Holland Tunnel links New York and New Jersey

1928 The Iron Lung, a chamber to force air in and out of the lungs is used on a polio patient

Alexander Fleming discovers penicillin

SPOTLIGHT ON THE WORLD OF ENTERTAINMENT

1920 Writers of the times met daily at "The Algonquin Round Table," in Manhattan's Algonquin Hotel

Hugh Lofting, writes *The Story of Doctor Doolittle* about a doctor who talks to animals

1921 Actor Rudolph Valentino's, *The Sheik,* brought passion to the silent screen and female hearts

Composer, Irving Berlin writes *April Showers*

1922 T.S. Eliot publishes *The Waste Land*, this poem represents American feeling after the war

1923 Flappers were dancing the newest craze, the *Charleston*

The Roar that Fizzled

1924 George Gershwin composes *Rhapsody in Blue,* a mix of classical and jazz for a concert hall

Little Orphan Annie, a comic strip by Harold Gray, debuts in the New York Daily News

1925 F. Scott Fitzgerald's *The Great Gatsby,* is a sign of the times showing the desire for wealth

Sinclair Lewis's *Arrowsmith* which criticizes the medical profession wins the Pulitzer Prize

Jazz gains popularity

1926 Ernest Hemingway's *The Sun Also Rises,* telling a tale in Europe after World War I, is published

A.A. Milne's *Winnie the Pooh,* is about a bear who gets in trouble and always learns a lesson

BOOK-OF-THE-MONTH CLUB is begun by Harry Scherman

1927 Singer, Al Jolson stars in the first talking movie, *The Jazz Singer*

1928 Al Jolson's *Sonny Boy* sells over 12 million records

The first cartoon featuring sound, *Steamboat Willy*, starring Mickey Mouse, is released

1929 James Joyce's *Ulysses* is published amid controversy over the language

A Farewell to Arms depicts Hemingway's observations as an ambulance driver during World War I

SPORTS' HIGHLIGHTS

1920 George Herman "Babe" Ruth is sold by the Boston Red Sox to the New York Yankees

Cooperstown, N.Y. becomes a baseball field memorial

1921 First play-by-play broadcast of baseball World Series Game

The U.S. Tennis team wins the Davis Cup

Spitball is banned from baseball after batter Ray Chapman is struck and killed by the pitch

1924 Rogers Hornsby bats .424, the highest average ever in modern baseball

1925 The Notre Dame Fighting Irish, led by coach Knute Rockne, defeat Stanford in the Rose Bowl

1926 Gene Tunney, defeats William "Jack" Dempsey to become Heavyweight Boxing Champion

1927 Babe Ruth hits 60 home runs in one season

OTHER INTERESTING FACTS

1920 First Air-Mail flight, New York to San Francisco

BABY RUTH candy bars, named after Grover Cleveland's daughter, are introduced

First GOOD HUMOR ice cream trucks, bring ice cream direct to neighborhood streets

WHEATIES, a breakfast cereal, is introduced with the slogan, "the breakfast of champions"

REESE'S PEANUT BUTTER CUPS, candy mixing chocolate and peanut butter are created

1921 Former President, William H. Taft, becomes Chief Justice of the Supreme Court

The first Miss America pageant is held

Americans spend over $10 million on radio sets and parts

1924 J. Edgar Hoover, becomes Director of the Bureau of Investigation

Insecticides are used for the first time

Mah Jongg, imported from China becomes a popular game craze

1925 Chrysler Corporation is started by Walter Chrysler

Nellie Ross, of Wyoming, becomes the first woman elected governor in the U.S.

The first national spelling bee is hosted by the Louisville Courier Journal

THE JOLLY GREEN GIANT first appears on canned vegetables

Homogenized milk, processed as to not separate the milk and cream is introduced by Borden

RICE KRISPIES, cereal that says snap, crackle and pop when mixed with milk is introduced

Daniel Gerber begins marketing his wife's concept for strained baby foods

1926 Kodak produces the first 16mm movie film

Gertrude Ederle of U.S. is the first woman to swim the English Channel

The Roar that Fizzled

1927 Charles A. Lindbergh, first to fly the Atlantic solo, non-stop flight from New York to Paris

WONDER BREAD, the first pre-sliced bread, is introduced by the Continental Baking Company

1929 First YO-YO, a spool like toy attached with a string to spin up and down is marked by D. Duncan

Hostess TWINKIES, a snack size, white cake with a fluffy cream center is created

FRITOS, tortilla chips are created by Elmer Doolin

The shopping cart is invented to enable customers to buy more items

SARA LEE ORIGINAL CHEESE CAKE, a cake made with real cream cheese is introduced

REYNOLDS WRAP, an aluminum foil for storing leftovers is introduced

Introduction to the Decade

Following the end of World War I, Americans were ready to get on with building a nation of prosperity. By the early twenties the manufacture of post-war materials resulted in a booming economy. Symbols of the times such as automobiles and new furnishings for the home become easier to acquire.

Adults wanted to forget the war years and just enjoy life and play. The motion picture and sports industries provided them with exciting pastimes. The rhythm and beat of Jazz heralded in an era of fun with few restrictions in dress, manners and morals. "Flappers," described women with bobbed hair who danced the "Charleston" and "Black Bottom," vigorously, while the fringes and beads of their short dresses flapped. They smoked cigarettes and wore flashy make-up and were escorted by men with "bowler" or felt brimmed hats and suits of color and design that broke away from the conservative black of previous times. Playing the stock market and enjoying the good times, was the way of life.

There were also millions of families from the farms of the mid-west to the tenements of the big cities—unaffected by the changes around them. Their chief concern was making a modest living and raising their children. What the children had was creativity, inspiration and the desire to have fun, which they turned into innovative games. Lou Baum, was one of those children who used his creativity in the streets, and continued to express his creativity in his writings which he started in elementary school. Writing poetry and short stories, Baum found a place for his expression and during the war years continued to write letters about his experiences. Over the years, while devoting time to work, his wife and family, he still found time to write. In 1999, at eighty-two years of age, Lou was still writing and working on his novel, "Tenement Tales." Lou Baum allowed us a preview of what life was like during those years, by giving us a glimpse into the tenements of New York as seen through the eyes of a young boy playing his "Street Games."

Street Games

Lou Baum

In many households during the 'Roaring Twenties' there were lots of worries and problems, economic problems mostly. Occasionally, some kids got to go to the movie houses, that held no interest for me. My days were completely taken up with street games.

Before I could go out and play, I had to do chores. One of my chores was to empty the "Ice Box" basin twice a day. The "Ice Box" was used in kitchens throughout tenement districts to keep food cold. Inside these units was a special space set aside for a large piece of ice that kept the food from spoiling. We placed a big basin under each "Ice Box," to catch the water drippings. I always seemed to manage to empty the basin out just in time. A few minutes more and the whole kitchen would have been flooded. I would lift the heavy water filled basin and take it over to the sink. Dumping the water made a big loud splash and in the morning I had to go slow as it might awaken my father. With that done I could go out and play our street games.

Once the sun was up you could find all the neighborhood kids in the street and speaking for myself, all my cares just vanished. The girls liked to jump rope using clothes line; two girls would turn the rope while one attempted to jump over without stepping on it.

The younger boys played, hide and seek; one person counted while everyone else hid. At the end of the count that person tried to find the others and the one found becomes "it," then that person started to count, while everyone hid. These were the easy games. But we older boys played more manly games. Here are a few of my favorites:

Ring-A-Lee-Veo

One kid would be "It" and would chase and try to grab one of the other kids. When someone was caught, the one who was "It" would have to hold on to his prey until he could say Ring-a-lee-veo three times. The grabbed kid obviously would try to escape; clothes were torn, fingernails dug into skin, and sometimes there was a little blood and a few scratches. All this violence was because the one who was caught would then become "It."

Johnny on a Pony

A game that we played for a long, long time even as we grew older was called Johnny on a Pony, well known in any tenement district. All that was needed was a strong wall. One husky fellow to stand with his back against the side of a building. Three or four others would bend over half way from the waist, holding onto the waist of the one in front, making a chain. When it looked like the back of a pony each kid would take a turn jumping on and the ones who formed the pony had to keep from falling down, while having these kids sitting on their backs. Eventually someone would jump on and the pony would cave in taking all its riders with it.

Punch Ball

Punch ball, which was played with a Spaulding ball and your fist, had an element of risk. A playing field was established on the road with each player taking up a position. When a fly ball was punched into the outfield, most of the time, it would be headed toward the cellars in the tenements. The kid playing the outfield would try to catch the ball. Sometimes he would keep going back, winding up down the cellar steps. Sometimes he would stumble, trip over the steps, and end up with a bruise or two, or even a sprained ankle.

Fire Hydrants

On very hot summer days, the city would open the hydrants so that the kids could prance and fool around in the water trying to cool off.

Some kids would slide on the flume of water and end up piled and jumbled in the street. Occasionally some wise aleck would stand right in front of the hydrants opening and the force of the water would be so powerful, it would send the kid literally flying. It was really quite dangerous.

Winter Sports

We also had winter sports. Nope, not skiing, although we did have our own version of a sliding pond.

The Water Slide

We would borrow pans from the candy store and ask the owner to fill them with water which we then spilled on the street from one sewer to the other—which was quite a distance. Then we'd wait until the street froze over and became a sheet of ice. Kids would start by running a few steps and then sliding as far as they could go. This was another opportunity for cuts and bruises.

Snow Ball War

After a big snow fall we would build forts on both sides of the street, from the gathered snow that piled up against the curbs when the plows came through. From the forts we would stage Snowball Wars. We would also dig holes in the snow banks then cover them up with newspapers or cardboard. Then invent some kind of game like "try to catch me" to entice other kids to follow us. We'd jump over the traps, but they would fall in and get soaking wet. Of course everybody had a big laugh, except those who fell in.

Playin' for Pennies

Thinking about risks reminds me how great the risk was when we decided to gamble for pennies because it was against the law. The cop on the beat would sometimes sneak up and catch us, and whack us with his club stick. We were never sure if we would be arrested for gambling.

Intermission

When we kids got hungry, hot and perspiring, we'd stand in front of our building facing our apartment windows and yell up to our mothers, "Throw down money." Mother would carefully wrap whatever loose change she could find in a kerchief, tie it tightly and toss it out the window. Sometimes we'd make a great catch, other times—we'd search the street until we found the money. Then we'd run to the candy store where for two cents you could get fountain sodas, made from syrup and seltzer, egg creams which were milk, seltzer and chocolate syrup that cost five cents, or malted's, which were expensive, but worth it at ten cents. They came in a variety of flavors and were made with milk, your favorite ice cream and malted powder. The mixture was put in a blender and it came out thick and frothy. On a hot day "eskimo pie's," chocolate coating wrapped around vanilla ice cream, were a popular five cent treat.

After the break, the kids would just keep on playing and playing until the end of the day when dusk would fall, reminding them they had a home to go to.

Thinking back, I fully realize and appreciate all the good days and happy times I had in those years. Playing those street games, some known, some made up in the spur of the moment, we had a marvelous time.

The Roar that Fizzled

Conclusion of the Decade

The turbulence of the twenties was making it harder and harder for families to shut out the realities of their world. The flamboyant years had simmered down quickly and by the end of the decade, all Americans, including the children were experiencing a very different life. Widespread unemployment and poverty were seen on the streets as breadlines grew and children became part of the sparse labor force to help support their families. "Sweatshops," became a place for cheap labor, employing children and adults desperate to earn even the smallest wage; often employing practices of unfair labor in unsafe conditions. As the world economy plummeted down many had to turn to "soup kitchens" for their next meal. Although times were hard, some were able to squeeze out an extra nickel or dime, to buy a ticket to a movie and for a few hours, get lost in the extravaganza of a world they could only dream about.

1930's

4

And The World Goes Down and Down

1930-1939

*The Great Depression brought the worst of times,
    but Americans kept their hopes alive
    with their music, radio and movies.*

Memorable Events of the Decade

PRESIDENTS AND THEIR FIRST LADIES

1930–1933 31st   Herbert Hoover   First Lady Lou Henry
1933–1939 32nd   Franklin D. Roosevelt   First Lady Eleanor Roosevelt

MAJOR EVENTS OF THE UNITED STATES AND WORLD HISTORY

1932   Mohandas Gandhi fasts for self-rule in India

Depression takes its toll on Americans

1933   Prohibition of alcohol is repealed

United Soviet Socialist Republic recognized by U.S.

President Roosevelt begins New Deal, his programs to combat the depression

A drought in middle America turns the farmland into "The Dust Bowl"

1934   Adolf Hitler becomes German Führer (leader)—Nazi Party comes to power

Our nation's first general strike

The Federal Bureau of Investigations (FBI), a government crime fighting force is created

1935   Roosevelt signs the Social Security Act, a federal pension system for the elderly

Fascist Italian dictator, Benito Mussolini, conquers Ethiopia

1936   Farmers leave their land as mother nature spreads her dust storms

Fascist, Francisco Franco begins a civil war in Spain

1937   The United Auto Worker's successfully strike against General Motors

Japan invades China at Peking, in what is called the first battle of World War II

1938   Germany Invades Austria

Nazis raid Jewish homes, businesses and synagogues—called Kristallnacht—Night of Broken Glass

Fair Labor Standards Act fixes minimum wage at 40 cents an hour and 40 hour work week

And The World Goes Down and Down

1939 World War II begins—Germany invades Poland—France and Great Britain declare war on Germany.

IMPORTANT ADVANCES IN SCIENCE AND TECHNOLOGY

1930 Astronomer Clyde Tombaugh discovers the planet Pluto

1931 Harold C. Urey discovers heavy hydrogen

1935 Charles Richter invents the Richter Scale, a scale used to measure earthquake intensity

1936 Boulder Dam on the Colorado River creates Lake Mead, the largest reservoir in the world

1937 First use of insulin to control diabetes

Nylon, the first manufactured fiber is patented by Du Pont chemist Wallace H. Carothers

1938 TEFLON, a polymer used in non-stick coating and fiberglass, glass woven into textiles are invented

Scientists begin to suspect that smoking causes lung cancer

Chester Carlson makes the first photocopy, and invents xeroxing

L. Biro makes the first functional ballpoint pen

1939 Edwin Armstrong invents FM (frequency modulation)

DDT, the first modern chemical pesticide, is developed by Paul Muller, a Swiss chemist

Official debut of television at the World's Fair

First jet plane takes off

SPOTLIGHT ON THE WORLD OF ENTERTAINMENT

1930 Grant Wood's *American Gothic*, paints the vanishing rural life-style

Sinclair Lewis becomes the first American to win the Nobel Prize for literature

Comic strip *Blondie* debuts, as husband Dagwood is always getting in and out of trouble

Motion picture houses replace the entertainment of Vaudeville theatres

1931 The Palace in New York is the only remaining large Vaudeville house in the country

1932 Songwriter, E.Y."Yip" Harburg's *Brother Can You Spare A Dime?* depicts the Depression

1933 *King Kong*, a story about a gorilla and a girl, which uses special effects is a big hit at the movies

Dancers Fred Astaire and Ginger Rogers are first paired

Critic Gertrude Stein's *Autobiography of Alice B. Toklas*, is believed to chronicle her life

1935 George Gershwin's opera *Porgy and Bess* written for an all black cast, opens in New York

The *Rumba* becomes the dance in fashion

Benny Goodman's music, a new style of jazz, called *Swing*, becomes popular

1936 Dale Carnegie's *How To Win Friends and Influence People* explains how to be popular

Margaret Mitchell's, *Gone With the Wind* is about the pre and post Civil War South

Life magazine begins publication, telling the story of life in articles and pictures

8-year-old Shirley Temple is an acting, singing, dancing superstar

1937 Disney introduces *Snow White and the Seven Dwarfs*, a cartoon movie

Bugs Bunny makes his cartoon debut in *Porky's Hare Hunt*

1938 Two high school friends create the comic book hero *Superman*, "The Man of Steel"

Ella Fitzgerald, black, blues singer has her first hit

Orson Welles's broadcast of H.G. Wells's *War of the Worlds* is believed to be an alien invasion

1939 David O. Selznick premiers *Gone with the Wind,* a motion picture extravaganza

The Wizard of Oz, mixes black and white and color to present the real and the dreamed

Painter Anna Mary Robertson Moses, a.k.a. Grandma Moses, becomes famous at age 79

POCKET BOOKS creates the first paperback novels

SPORTS' HIGHLIGHTS

1930 Super Golfer, Bobby Jones wins U.S. and British Open and British Amateur

And The World Goes Down and Down

1932 Heavyweight boxer Jack Sharkey (U.S.) defeats Max Schmeling (Ger.) to win world title

1933 First baseball All-Star Game played

1934 Max Baer wins world heavyweight boxing title

1936 U.S. track superstar Jesse Owens, earns four gold medals at the Olympics in Berlin

Boxer Max Schmeling, represents Hitler's theory of white supremacy when he defeats black boxer Joe Louis

1938 In a rematch Joe Louis defeats Hitler's Max Schmeling, in the first round

1939 First televised baseball game

The New York Yankees win their fourth consecutive World Championship

New York Yankees' Lou Gehrig retires from baseball after being struck by a fatal disease

OTHER INTERESTING FACTS

1930 U.S. Population—122 million

Gangster Al Capone sentenced to 11 years in prison for tax evasion

Bridge becomes a popular card game

Ellen Church, a nurse, becomes the first airline stewardess, when she takes care of passengers

KING KULLEN, the first supermarket, a huge open space where customers pick their purchases

C. Darrow's **MONOPOLY**, a board game of real estate and finance uses Atlantic City street names

1931 *The Star Spangled Banner* becomes the official U.S. Anthem

George Washington Bridge between New York and New Jersey is completed

Empire State Building, the world's tallest building opens

George Gallup, a journalism professor, conducts the first Gallup Poll, asking people's opinions

1932 Amelia Earhart is the first woman to fly the Atlantic solo

The first parking meters are installed in Oklahoma City

1935 Alcoholics Anonymous is started in New York to help with the problem of alcoholism

1934 The Dionne quintuplets are born

1936 The *Hindenberg,* a hydrogen filled airship explodes while landing at Lakehurst, New Jersey

1937 Amelia Earhart and her navigator are lost somewhere in Pacific on round-the-world flight.

1939 Einstein writes FDR about the feasibility of the atomic bomb
World's Fair opens in New York

Introduction to the Decade

Following the crash of the stock market in 1929, the decade of the thirties dawned bleak and seemingly hopeless for millions of Americans. Banks went broke, factories and businesses shut down and millions of people were unemployed. Economic chaos engulfed the nation and farmers by the thousands, especially in the Mid-West lost their land due to dust storms. In the literary corner, John Steinbeck's Pulitzer Prize winning novel, "The Grapes of Wrath," graphically portrayed these hardships. By the time President Franklin D. Roosevelt was elected, war clouds had begun to gather in Europe, but the United States would not enter World War II until the forties. Roosevelt trying to stem the economic tide established "The New Deal." Americans needed an escape and the movie houses flourished. Disney's cartoon character "Mickey Mouse" and the singing, dancing child star, "Shirley Temple" became household names. Americans could go to the movies or gather around their radios to keep abreast of world news and to enjoy various programs.

As a child growing into a young women, Bobbi R. Madry experienced first-hand the courage of so many families during the depression and those who gave generously to help the less fortunate. Families enjoyed time together and it was that family spirit that helped them to face all the adversities of the times. This made a lasting impression on Bobbi and through the years she went on to realize her goals of becoming an author. She served as author and senior editor of educational publications and director of human relations programs for major New York City publishers. In 1998 Bobbi became Educational Director of The Write Source and Golden Quill Press.

I Remember Charlie

Bobbi R. Madry

Ellie and I pulled the heavy hand-made quilt over us to keep warm and to muffle our giggles. It was way past bed time for little girls even if it was New Years Eve of 1930, a brand new decade and grownups were celebrating. I was six and Ellie was seven, yet we understood most of what we heard grownups talking about, especially how bad the twenties had been and how the Stock Market crash of 1929, had affected just about every family. But Ellie and I couldn't imagine people going hungry or standing in bread lines to get a meal.

As this new decade dawned we'd heard about the depression, fortunately, our families weren't severely affected by it. Stores in our town were doing fine so far; the butcher, hardware, bakery, fish and furniture store all were able to stay in business and keep the silent ethics of not selling something their neighbor sold. Ellie's dad owned a grocery store, but his main problem was he couldn't say no to needy families who had to charge their groceries. The store stocked a little of everything from canned goods to bins of rice, beans and bushels of potatoes and apples. The store had a long counter with a hand-operated cash register that looked more like a typewriter. On one end was a scale with a large roll of brown wrapping paper, paper bags and a large roll of string. You came in with your grocery list and Ellie's dad and her brother Charlie, age nine, would get your items off the shelf, or from the containers, add up the total price, usually writing the prices on a paper sack, and then bag all your groceries. Then they would carry it out to your car or Charlie would deliver small orders by bicycle. His Dad would deliver big grocery orders just to show off his bright, new Chevy Roadster with a rumble seat; an open seat in the rear of the car, behind the roof, which could be folded shut when it wasn't being used. And what fun it was to ride in that rumble seat, with the wind blowing in our hair. If it started raining we'd have to hunker down and pull the back of the rumble seat over us to stay dry.

I liked visiting with Ellie. Her parents house was decorated in the new thirties art-deco style. There was a lot of mirrored glass, fabrics of bold patterns and colors and a real bear rug adorned the highly polished wooden floors. The furniture looked sleek and modern, with rounded edges, chrome trim and shiny surfaces. The decor was considered "arty." There was no way to compare it to our old style farmhouse furniture, made of wood. We called it American style, meaning more useable than anything else.

Ellie's family, her Dad, Mom and brother Charlie lived in a small town about two miles from where I lived with my Aunt Julie and Uncle Jay who had become my guardians after the death of my parents when I was only a toddler. It was called a "Truck Farm," a small farm that produced and supplied a variety of fruits and vegetables to area stores and for visitors to our fruit stand during the growing season. At the end of the season, my uncle would invite needy area families with their children to come to the orchards and pick whatever they wanted for free. He made sure there were plenty of pumpkins available for Halloween. He would also use his old pick-up truck to deliver to stores and people who couldn't get to the farm. We used that old truck for everything—we even drove it to church.

The farm house kitchen was a busy place. My aunt cooked on a wood-burning stove and at canning time when she'd be busy putting up preserves, fruits and vegetables, I got the job of washing the jars. I didn't like it much, but kept telling myself those fruits would taste great in the winter.

When I wasn't helping my aunt I was with Ellie. We did everything together; school, dance lessons, parties, playing games and sleeping over at one another's homes. We loved going to the movies on Saturdays and we especially loved the musicals, starring, the great dancing pair, Fred Astaire and Ginger Rogers. We were entranced by the musical extravaganzas with their big production numbers featuring hundreds of beautiful dancing girls in their magnificent costumes. When we'd come home we'd play dress up with fancy clothes of satin and chiffon that Ellie's Mom passed along to us, then we'd practice our tap dancing, pretending we were dancing girls.

We would spend hours watching Ellie's mom bleach her hair platinum so she'd be in style with such movie stars as Jean Harlow and Mae West. We were fascinated watching her arch her eyebrows in a high, thin line, she said gave her a Greta "Garbo" look—a style named for the mysterious, Swedish actress.

My only problem during those early years of the thirties was Charlie who liked to pull my hair ribbons off the ends of my long braids. He called himself "Dick Tracy," ace detective after the comic strip character. Another time he'd pretend to be "The Lone Ranger," the masked man from radio who with his faithful Indian sidekick would help people and then ride off into the sunset. Charlie would pester us while we tried to listen to our favorite music. Some of the fun songs Ellie and I liked were "Roll Out the Barrel," "Easter Parade, " or we'd put on a show when we sang Shirley Temple's, "On The Good Ship Lollipop." But Charlie didn't like being ignored and sometimes he'd sneak up on us like "Frankenstein," hovering and making grunting noises, the same way actor Boris Karloff did it in the movies. Boy were we scared.

As the years rolled by life began to take on a different meaning. Ellie and I were becoming young women. We whispered a lot about things our parents seemed too embarrassed to talk about. Our sex education was one word. No! It was about that time my relationship with Ellie began to change. She fell in love with a boy named Robbie, who was into sports and that was about all she was interested in. Among his heroes were U.S. Track superstar Jesse Owens, who earned four Gold Medals at the Olympics in Berlin and New York Yankees, Babe Ruth and Lou Gehrig who lead their team to World Championships during that time.

I didn't mind spending time alone. I would spend it reading and devouring books and magazines. I loved Life magazine and such books as, Pearl Buck's, "The Good Earth," Robert Frost's, "Collected Poems," "Maxwell Anderson's, "Elizabeth, The Queen," Agatha Christie's, "Ten Little Indians," but my favorite was Margaret Mitchell's, "Gone With The Wind." The more I read the more I knew I wanted to be a writer.

It was about that same time that I noticed Charlie acting strange when he was around me. He wanted to hang around my house and with me at the movies. He loved the outdoors and when he wasn't helping his dad, he'd mow lawns to earn extra money, or come out to the farm and help me pick strawberries.

Then one night when I was about fifteen, he asked if I'd go to the school dance with him. This was the first time I really noticed that skinny kid had developed great looking muscles. He had devilishly twinkly brown eyes, a crooked grin with one slightly crooked tooth and his golden brown hair had a wave that always parted over his eyebrow.

The night of the dance, I felt so pretty in the dress Aunt Julie made for me. It was a pale lavender, silk organdy, with a lace trimmed ruffle framing my shoulders. It had a wide sash with a butterfly bow in the back and another ruffle trimmed the floor length skirt. By this time I thought I should give up my pig-tails, so Gladys, the local beautician cut my hair to shoulder length, parted it to the side and set it in soft, flowing, finger waves. Back in those days, nice girls didn't wear make-up, but we did pinch our cheeks for color and were allowed on special occasions to wear pale pink lipstick.

Charlie looked so handsome when he came to call for me in his dark suit, white shirt and dark blue bowtie. By then he had his own Model A car, a two door, four-seater that he fixed up himself. It was a fairy tale evening and Charlie got me home on time.

He was my first date and my first real kiss. That night I wrote in my diary, "Charlie, XXX," meaning I Love You. I even pressed a camellia from my corsage between the pages of Edna St. Vincent Millay's Sonnets.

As time marched on, Charlie and I began to talk about "what if," after college, when he took over his fathers' business and I got my journalism degree so I could start our own area newspaper. But our "what if's" had to be put on hold. By the end of the thirties war clouds had been gathering in Europe and many nights we were glued to the radio listening to President Franklin Roosevelt's Fireside Chats—but it couldn't happen to us. Charlie and I were sure we would have the future we planned. It never occurred to us to by-pass our family traditions of school, job, home and then marriage, in that order. He gave me his class ring and I gave him my treasured medallion, a pearl that represented my birth stone. We pledged our secret pact, that New Years Eve of 1939, as we danced together to, "When You Wish Upon A Star." We couldn't know that soon—far too soon, kids like us, not old enough to vote, not old enough to marry, would be old enough to face the horrors that World War II would bring. I was so proud of Charlie when I saw him in his uniform, never realizing . . . some would come back . . . some would not . . . and some of us would face the future with only our memories . . . and I remember Charlie.

Conclusion of the Decade

By the end of the depressed thirties some of the programs introduced to relieve unemployment and put the economy back on its feet began taking effect. Prohibition was gone and the escape mechanism of movies went from black and white to full color mimicking the mood of the country, as it came from the deepest depression to a time of gaining back its economic strength. The "Star Spangled Banner" became our national anthem and love of country became our theme. But there was still much anxiety. The news from Europe brought fears that we would once again be drawn into war . . . but we continued to hope that our country would remain at peace and our shores would remain safe.

1940's

5

Marching To War...
Bonds, Rationing...
A People United

1940-1949

To sacrifice and fight for our country . . .
to preserve our cherished freedom.

Memorable Events of the Decade

PRESIDENTS AND THEIR FIRST LADIES

1940 – 1945 32nd Franklin D. Roosevelt   First Lady Eleanor Roosevelt
1945 – 1949 33rd Harry S. Truman   First Lady Bess Wallace

MAJOR EVENTS OF THE UNITED STATES AND WORLD HISTORY

1940 Germany defeats France—begins "Blitzkreig," bombing civilian targets in Great Britain

Winston Churchill becomes Prime Minister of England

1941 Sunday morning, December 7, Japanese surprise attack the naval base on Pearl Harbor, Hawaii

United States declares war on the Japanese and enters World War II

Hitler, doomed to make the same mistake as Napoleon, enters Russia

1942 Japanese-Americans are herded into internment camps

Manhattan Project scientists develop the atomic bomb

U.S. victory in the Battle of Midway shifts the war in the Pacific in favor of the Allies

General Douglas MacArthur vows "I will return," after he's ordered to leave the Philippines

1943 German army suffers defeat at the hands of the Soviets

1944 D-Day begins as the allies land in Normandy—the end of the war is near

Germany takes last stand at the Battle of the Bulge

The G.I. Bill of Rights is signed by President Roosevelt

1945 Roosevelt, Churchill and Stalin meet at Yalta to discuss post-war Europe

1945 Germany surrenders—Hitler believed to have committed suicide

B29 named the Enola Gay drops the atomic bomb on Hiroshima, Japan—80,000 dead

Three days later—second bomb is dropped on Nagasaki

August 10, the Japanese surrender—World War II is over

The Nuremberg Trials, a military tribunal held in Germany exposes crimes of the holocaust

50 nations charter the United Nations, setting goals for peace, human social and economic rights

1946 The "Iron Curtain" goes up in Europe dividing the continent into free and communist rule

1947 Secretary of State Marshall outlines The Marshall Plan to put war torn Europe back on its feet

The United Nations partitions British-controlled Palestine into Jewish-Arab states

1948 The Jewish State of Israel is born—President Truman pledges U.S. support

1948 NATO, the North Atlantic Treaty Organization is established to stem the tide of Communism

Western allies airlift supplies to West Berlin as Soviets blockade the city

1949 Mao Zedong defeats Chiang Kai-shek's Nationalists beginning the Communist regime of China

IMPORTANT ADVANCES IN SCIENCE AND TECHNOLOGY

1940 Igor Sikorsky designs and pilots the first successful helicopter, a single blade flying machine

Plutonium, a radioactive metallic chemical element is discovered

1941 The United States begins regular television broadcasts

1942 Physicist Enrico Fermi achieves the first nuclear chain reaction

Magnetic recording tape invented

The first electronic digital calculator is developed; cost $500 million and weight 35 tons

1944 Streptomycin is developed as an antibiotic that fights bacterial infection

Oswald Avery discovers that genetic material is made up of deoxyribonucleic acid (DNA)

1945 First atomic bomb which uses plutonium as an explosive is detonated New Mexico

1946 *ENIAC* (Electronic Numerical Integrator and Computer) is the first Computer

1947 Test pilot, 24-year-old Chuck Yeager, flies at 700 miles per hour breaking the sound barrier

1948 Bell Laboratories' transistor, is a smaller, faster, cheaper way to regulate electric current

The first Polaroid camera, which develops pictures instantly, is introduced by Edwin Land

SPOTLIGHT ON THE WORLD OF ENTERTAINMENT

1940 *Batman,* a caped crusader, makes his first comic book appearance

Walt Disney's *Fantasia,* mixes cartoons with classical music

For Whom The Bell Tolls, recounts Hemingway's adventures in the Spanish Civil War

1941 *Citizen Kane* produced and starring Orson Welles tells the story of power driven newspaper magnate

Margaret and H.H. Rey publish the first *Curious George* book about the misadventures of a monkey

1942 Humphrey Bogart and Ingrid Bergman star in *Casablanca,* a story of love, espionage and loyalty

Frank Sinatra tugs at teenage girls' heartstrings when he makes his solo debut

1944 A plane transporting band leader Glenn Miller across the Atlantic disappears

Bebop, improvisational jazz—developed by Charlie Parker, Dizzy Gillespie and Thelonius Monk

1946 Jimmy Stewart gets his wish in *It's a Wonderful Life,* when he wishes he were never born

1947 Suspicions of communism come to the movies as the "Hollywood Ten" are blacklisted

1948 Television, bringing pictures to your living room in a box, becomes an integral part of American life

The LP, or long-playing phonograph record, is introduced by Columbia Records

1949 George Orwell publishes his futurist look at *1984*

Arthur Miller's Broadway debut of *Death of a Salesman,* tells the story of Willie Loman

Miles Davis introduces "Cool Jazz," a more laid back type of jazz

Marching To War . . . Bonds, Rationing . . . A People United   57

SPORTS' HIGHLIGHTS

1941 Yankee Joe DiMaggio hits safely, getting at least one hit, in 56 consecutive games

Baseball's great "Iron Man," Lou Gehrig dies

Baseball's Ted Williams bats .406

1945 Rocky Graziano is the boxer of the year

1945 Jockey Eddie Arcaro wins with *Whirlaway* at the Kentucky Derby, Preakness and Belmont

1946 The National Basketball Association is founded

1947 Jackie Robinson, the first black man in major league baseball, wins "Rookie of the Year"

1948 "Pancho" Gonzales emerges as U.S. Tennis star

Jockey Eddie Arcaro riding *Citation* wins the Triple Crown

OTHER INTERESTING FACTS

1940 U.S. Population tops 131.6 million people

Nylons are first sold in the United States

Selective Service Act, compulsory military service determined by age and other criteria is signed

M&M candies are developed by Forrest Mars and Bruce Murrie

1941 Congresswomen Jeannette Rankin casts the only "No" vote to declare war on Japan after Pearl Harbor

1942 Women's military services established

The F.B.I. captures eight Nazi saboteurs from a submarine off Long Island Sound in New York

"G.I. Joe" is coined in a cartoon by Lieutenant Dave Gerger, meaning "government issue"

1943 President freezes prices, salaries and wages to prevent inflation

Income tax withholding is introduced

THE ZOOT SUIT, oversized suit with narrowed at the ankle trousers is the latest fashion fad

Foot stomping and gyrations release war tensions as *The Jitterbug* becomes the dance craze

The Pentagon, the world's largest office building, is completed

1944 G.I. Bill of Rights is passed, gives returning soldiers low income housing and college scholarships

1945 Grand Rapids, Michigan becomes the first city to begin fluoridation of its water supply

1946 First meeting of the United Nations General Assembly

1947 French fashion designer Christian Dior unveils his "New Look"

The Dead Sea Scrolls, information about the Hebrew Bible are found

Marching To War . . . Bonds, Rationing . . . A People United

INTRODUCTION TO THE DECADE

As we entered the forties, although mindful of the war raging in Europe and fearful that the United States would eventually become involved, it took the attack on Pearl Harbor, by the Japanese, on December 7, 1941, to jolt America awake to what lay ahead. As the country mobilized, men and women by the thousands left their jobs and families to join the military forces. Women not only kept the home fires burning, they took on jobs that helped to move the nation to victory. When the war ended in 1945, the main concern was getting the troops home and the wheels of progress turning again. After war years of shortages and rationing, families hungered for homes, cars, appliances and other consumers goods.

In the forties while war raged around them at home, families tried to keep as much "normalcy" as possible. In 1999, Eileen M. Foti, a Tappan, New York resident, and the mother of three children remembered that time as she sat in her very busy household with her husband Charlie and their two Scotties, Kiltie and MacGregor, about whom she has written a fascinating book. An artist and an award winning photographer, her paintings and photographs have been included in numerous shows. In her story "A Look To The Past," Eileen remembers her childhood and how she learned about animals and their care while vacationing on a farm. Her family was able to experience a simplistic way of life that was untouched by the realities of war and Americans dying to protect that very way of life.

A Look to the Past

Eileen M. Foti

In the early 1940's, in another part of the world, World War II was being fought and the United States was drawn into the conflict when the Japanese bombed Pearl Harbor, December 7, 1941. Men were dying in battles and families were being pulled apart by the horrors that only war can bring. People were being put to death, because of their beliefs. I was a child and not really connected to the war, nor its sufferings, except what I heard from adults. But, my most vivid memory of that time is of a place many miles from the war when I stood on a platform with my family awaiting a train which appeared huge and overwhelming. While waiting for the train, I would look down onto the tracks and my stomach would drop and my feet would tingle. I imagined falling on the tracks with the train coming. The large black train could be heard from quite a distance coming into the station. The whistle blew when the brakes were applied. The wheels scraped along the tracks until they came to a halt. As the train finally stopped, a man in uniform put down a small flight of stairs, "All aboard," he yelled. One by one the people climbed up the stairs and into the train. After we boarded the train, my fear was forgotten as we were seated in a compartment and I looked out of a large window. Many people rode this long, black train. Some carried bags but most had newspapers tucked under their arms with headlines that reported stories of the war.

Sterling, Pennsylvania was our destination. We passed many towns and cities, but they were not as built up as they are today. Mostly, I was interested in the farms and the cows grazing in pastures. My family lived in Brooklyn, a borough of New York City, so I was very drawn to the great outdoors that opened up before my eyes. As the scenery flew by, I knew the train was traveling at a fast rate of speed. The people on the train, as well as my mother, were dressed in plain, but serviceable clothes. The men wore suits with large lapels and cuffs on their pant legs; much different than the styles that were to come later. During the forties women wore straight fitting suits or floral dresses. Many wore their hair swept up on their heads ending with clusters of curls on top. Silk stockings were hard to come by during the war, (that was before nylon). These stockings were sheer with seams down the back and every woman turned around to check to make sure her seams were straight.

My family took this trip every summer to spend a few weeks at Frick's Farm. Mr. and Mrs. Frick were an elderly couple who had been born and raised in Pennsylvania. The farm was in the country surrounded by many trees and green grass and a little stream ran along side the farm. Frogs hopped on the moss that clung to the rocks along the banks while dragonflies flew just above the waterline. Small fish swam in the clear cold water and water bugs landed like pontoon boats on the surface of the stream. These were the days when the waters were clean.

The large wood frame house we stayed in had a porch that surrounded the entire front, with white wooden rocking chairs that moved back and forth on the old wood floors. A large red barn stood off to the side of the farmhouse. It housed a hay loft, where hay was kept to feed the horses and cows, stalls for horses, pitch forks to throw the hay with and other farm equipment. Chickens were plentiful on this farm and they clucked all day long! We helped Mr. Frick collect the eggs each day. Some of the eggs were white and some were brown. Mr. Frick always told us that the brown eggs gave us brown chickens, but we didn't believe him. Mr. Frick threw the chickens feed and they all flocked around. We didn't know this then, but they were fed better than some people in Europe

A country store was right down the road from the farm. It was a small wooden building with glass windows. Inside the windows were assorted cans of food and produce. We'd walk to the store for treats and I would buy a bag of candy cigarettes, candy bananas, and candy dots of pink, blue and yellow. The dots, also called candy buttons, came on strips of paper and when you bit them off, little pieces of paper wound up in your mouth. My brother, sister and I lined up in a row and took turns spitting the little balls of paper to see who could spit further.

Sometimes our friends would come to Frick's Farm with us. Johnny and Louie were twin boys, my brother's age, but we all played together. Some days we would play tag and run around like ants at a picnic. Other days we played stickball. We used the handle from a broom and a rubber ball for our game. We didn't have enough kids to make up a real game, but we enjoyed playing together just the same. One day as we went out to pick blueberries up on the hill behind the farmhouse, everything was calm and peaceful and then it happened. A huge, brown bull with large, thick, curved horns on his head was coming toward us. His nostrils flared, then he stood still for a moment before he made his move to come towards us, snorting as he ran. We all ran and made it through the gate, except for Louie, he just stood there frozen with fear. His face was pale and his knees were shaking. We were all shouting at him to run, but he couldn't move. Just then the bull stopped short. It started to kick the dirt and wave its tail, chasing the humming flies that attempted to land on its back. We yelled, "Run Louie." Louie woke up from his trance. He ran so fast that he couldn't stop at the gate. Instead he leaped over it; just short of the bull reaching Louie's britches. Louie ran until he came to the farmhouse, through the door and up to his room. He didn't come out the rest of the day. We were all a little subdued that night. The next day we were just about over the scare, but now were into telling stories, one bigger than the other.

"I saw that bull. No big deal!" said Johnny, Louie's twin.

"He wasn't that big," my brother Jack said.

"He didn't run so fast. Louie had plenty of time to get away," I said.

Louie said nothing.

We then decided to go for a walk. The road was pretty safe. Not too many people living in this area had cars, but large black cars, mostly Packards, were sometimes seen on the roads. You didn't see the large variety of car makes and the assortment of colors we have today, nor the many imports.

The dusty road rose up as we kicked small stones along. After walking for awhile we began to feel thirsty. Turning a bend in the road we saw a little waterfall. In front of the waterfall was a shiny metal cup. We rinsed it in the waterfall and all had a long drink. The water was crystal clear and refreshing. We then replaced the cup for the next thirsty wanderers to enjoy. Today we wouldn't even think of drinking from that cup!

The days on the farm passed too quickly. When it was time to leave, packing was a slow process for us. We didn't want our vacation to end. With all kinds of good byes, from smiles to tears, we bid farewell to Mr. and Mrs. Frick. We piled the bags into the old farm truck and off we went to the station, but this time I wasn't so afraid. We boarded the train carrying Superman comic books, tootsie roll candy and loads of memories.

Our hopes were high about returning next year for more summer fun, without the bull, of course. When I think back about those mostly happy summers, I can still see Mrs. Frick rocking on her front porch and Mr. Frick feeding the chickens. Being children we had no idea of the terrible war that was being waged abroad and all the heartaches it brought. We were not too touched by it, until we would see the daily newspaper and see some of the pictures of the devastation the war caused.

Shortly after that visit to the farm we heard the Frick's had died. We never had a chance to go back, but the chambers of our minds still hold the pictures of our youth. And yet, as an adult, I more fully understand the realities of those war years . . . and am grateful for the illusions of childhood. I remember being so afraid of the train and as I think about the farm my memory releases these images and allows me to go back for a look at the past.

Introduction to the Story

While Eileen Foti was a child visiting a typical American farm, Jean M. Olwell's father was overseas, fighting to protect our freedom to live and enjoy our lives as we choose. In 1999, Jean was a teaching assistant who enjoyed writing and reading and theater, Jean was born in New York City, and continued her father's spirit of freedom and love of country by using her free time as a volunteer. History will never recall all the deeds of heroism of the many outstanding men and women who served their country during World War, however, Jean M. Olwell's story reflects their courage and dedication to making our world a better place.

Recalling a Father and D-Day 1944

Jean M. Olwell

I am writing to share with you the story of a remarkable young soldier in World War II. His name is Sgt. John J. Olwell. He is my father. Sgt. Olwell was a member of the 1st Division, 16th Infantry Regiment, otherwise known as "The Big Red One." From 1942-1943, the 1st Division spearheaded the invasions of North Africa, Tunisia and Sicily; then they returned to England to prepare for D-day.

On the morning of June 6, 1944, then a private, John Olwell 25, was already a combat veteran. He had served five years in the army and was no stranger to warfare. He was familiar with raids on pillboxes, those low enclosed concrete and steel positions from which heavy guns were fired. But the morning of June 6, will forever be etched in his mind and those of his fellow servicemen. All around the boats, young men were being shot, incinerated and were drowning. Pvt. Olwell's courage is best described in his citation for the Silver Star, the nation's second-highest award: "For gallantry in action in the vicinity of Normandy, France, June 6, 1944. When heavy machine gunfire seriously wounded his section leader, while landing on the invasion beach, Sgt. Olwell, then private, immediately assumed command and directed the unloading of the raft. Then, under intense interlocking fire, he reorganized his men and led them through unchartered mine fields to a forward position from which he directed a successful assault on the hostile pillboxes. Sgt. Olwell's courage and initiative merits the highest praise of the service."

Later, Gen. Omar Bradley was quoted as saying, "Members of the 16th Regiment, 1st. Division, turned threatened catastrophe into glorious victory for the American Army."

In 1984, my father was interviewed by the Newark Star-Ledger, however, he neglected to mention another act of heroism he performed that day. While crossing the beach, a young soldier approached my father. Dad motioned for the boy to be quiet. A German gunner, trained to shoot at anyone giving orders, aimed at Pvt. Olwell. When the shot rang out, my father watched in horror as the boy's face was shattered, and he fell, mortally wounded. Despite knowing full well that the gunner would probably shoot him next, Pvt. Olwell hastened to administer morphine and stem the bleeding of the dying man.

My dad and his division made it inland the night of June 6th, and they knew the road to Berlin was going to be long and rough. Before the war was over, he was promoted to sergeant, awarded the Silver Star, the Bronze Star, twice, the Purple Heart, twice, and received many other medals.

Dad never bragged about his accomplishments. He spoke only of the horror of war and those who died. Once he mentioned having seen some survivors, emaciated, in a concentration camp. I asked, "Daddy, were they men or women?" Even though it had been fifty years, tears welled in his eyes, and he replied, "You couldn't tell."

The world must never forget—not the countless victims of the Holocaust, nor the brave servicemen and women who fought and died to bring freedom to all humanity.

Conclusion of the Decade

American servicemen and women came home to cheers as we turned our thoughts from war to peacetime. As part of this new beginning, we looked to being whole families again and to enjoying our homes with new exciting modern conveniences that would make our lives easier. As a nation we also looked forward to building a better way of life for all our citizens. But we also had responsibilities to other nations who looked to us for leadership. The United States and the Soviet Union had emerged from World War II as super powers, with different political philosophies; democracy versus communism, but both with the ability to blow up the entire world. As we entered the fifties this caused a cloud to hover over our country. It was called "The Cold War."

We dedicate this chapter to all the men and women who served our country during World War II to protect our shores and safeguard our country's freedom.

1950's

6

Fast Forwarding into the Fabulous Fifties . . . the Best of Times

1950-1959

A time for recovery, with hopes to continue the peace dearly won and move forward with dreams for a better future for all Americans.

Memorable Events of the Decade

PRESIDENTS AND THEIR FIRST LADIES

1950 – 1953 33rd Harry S. Truman   First Lady Bess Wallace
1953 – 1959 34th Dwight D. Eisenhower   First Lady Mary "Mamie" Geneva Doud

MAJOR EVENTS OF THE UNITED STATES AND WORLD HISTORY

1950 North Korea invades South Korea—President sends in U.S. troops

1952 Wisconsin Senator Joseph McCarthy leads a congressional investigation of Americans loyalties

1953 Armistice signed ending the Korean War

1954 *Brown v. Board of Education of Topeka* bans racial segregation in public schools

1955 Rosa Parks, a black woman, refuses to give up her seat on a segregated bus to a white man

The Warsaw Pact, a military alliance between the Soviet Union and its European allies is signed

1956 Congress passes Interstate Highway Bill

1957 Russians launch *Sputnik I,* first earth-orbiting satellite—the Space Age begins

1958 Army's Jupiter-C rocket fires the first U.S. earth satellite, *Explorer I,* into orbit

Nikita Khrushchev becomes Premier of Soviet Union

General Charles de Gaulle becomes Premier of France

China's "Great Leap Forward" modernization program results in famine and 20 million deaths

1959 Cuban President Batista resigns and flees—Fidel Castro takes over in a bloody coup

IMPORTANT ADVANCES IN SCIENCE AND TECHNOLOGY

1950 Antihistamines become remedy for colds and allergies

Fast Forwarding into the Fabulous Fifties ... the Best of Times

1951 The first electricity generated by nuclear fission is produced in Idaho Falls, Idaho

Microwave ovens are introduced

1952 The United States tests the first Hydrogen bomb

1953 Dr. Alfred Kinsey's books on human sexual behavior are best-sellers

A successful measles vaccine is developed

Lung Cancer is attributed to cigarette smoking

DNA's structure is discovered

IBM Corporation unveils the 701, its first electronic computer

1954 Dr. Jonas Salk perfects a polio vaccine

IBM's 305, *RAMAC* is the first computer to use disk drive storage

RCA produces the first color television

The Sony Corporation introduces the first transistor radio, a portable radio that runs on batteries

The U.S. Navy launches the *Nautilus,* the first atomic submarine

1957 Pacemaker, an electronic devise implanted in the body for electric stimulation of the heart is used

1958 NASA, National Aeronautics and Space Administration is established

Texas Instrument engineer, Jack Kilby, invents the microchip, an integrated circuit

1959 Nobel Prize to Americans Ochoa and Kornberg for synthesis of RNA and DNA

SPOTLIGHT ON THE WORLD OF ENTERTAINMENT

1950 "Cool Jazz" a mellow sound with instrumental solos, takes the place of Bebop, livelier jazz

Charles Schulz's *Peanuts* comic strip, features Charlie Brown, a boy and his dog Snoopy

1951 Teen Holden Caulfield is chronicled with blunt language in Salinger's *Catcher In The Rye*

I Love Lucy, a husband-wife with comedic antics premieres on television

1952 *Bwana Devil*, the first 3-D movie with lifelike special effects seen through tinted glasses

1953 Ian Fleming publishes his first James Bond novel, *Casino Royale*

1954 *The Wild One*, starring Marlon Brando, typifies rebellious teenagers

Mad Comics changes to *Mad Magazine* to avoid regulations by the Comic Code Authority

1955 Tennessee Williams provocative *Cat on a Hot Tin Roof* wins the Pulitzer Prize for Drama

Promotion for movie *The Seven Year Itch* is a life-size image of its star, Marilyn Monroe

Jim Henson, a college freshman, creates his first Muppets—life-like puppets with personalities

Rock Around the Clock by Bill Haley and the Comets, the first rock 'n' roll song to reach #1

1956 Rock 'n' roll, music evolving from rhythm and blues using electric guitars is the new craze

19-year-old singer, Elvis Presley gains popularity with his rock and blues style and gyrating hips

Prince Rainier of Monaco marries actress Grace Kelly

Allen Ginsberg's poem *Howl* is filled with black culture slang and harsh reality

1957 Jack Kerouac drops out of main stream society to travel and write *On The Road*

Leonard Bernstein's *West Side Story*, is a modern day Romeo and Juliet musical set in New York City

Dr. Seuss's *Cat in the Hat* uses a mischievous cat to entertain two bored children

1958 The Guggenheim Museum designed by Frank Lloyd Wright opens in New York City

Buddy Holly, Ritchie Valens, and the Big Bopper die in a plane crash

SPORTS' HIGHLIGHTS

1951 Jersey Joe Walcott wins the heavyweight boxing title

1952 Rocky Marciano knocks out Jersey Joe Wallcott and is the new world heavyweight champ

1953 Golfer, Ben Hogan wins the Masters' and U.S. Open

1954 Roger Bannister runs the mile in 3 minutes, 59.4 seconds, the first to break the 4 minute mark

Fast Forwarding into the Fabulous Fifties . . . the Best of Times

1955 Sugar Ray Robinson becomes middleweight boxing champ

1956 Boxing champ Rocky Marciano retires unbeaten

Yankee Don Larsen pitches a "perfect game," in the World Series

Floyd Patterson becomes the heavyweight boxing champ

1957 Baseball's New York Giants move to San Francisco and the Brooklyn Dodgers to Los Angeles

1958 Golfer Arnold Palmer wins his first Masters' Tournament

Football's Baltimore Colts defeat New York Giants in overtime, 23-17 called, "The Greatest Game Ever Played"

OTHER INTERESTING FACTS

1950 United States population—approximately 150 million people

1950 The Diners' Club card becomes the first modern credit card, accepted at multiple places

1951 Sugar FROSTED FLAKES, a sweetened corn cereal is introduced by Kellogg's

The frozen T.V. Dinner is designed by Swanson to be re-heated and eaten in front of the television

The first meeting of Weight Watchers, a support group to assist people in losing weight is held

1952 The Holiday Inn hotel chain is founded by Kemmons Wilson

1955 Disneyland opens in California

U.S. minimum wage is $1

Davy Crockett coonskin caps become the rage

POGO STICKS, stilts with pedals for your feet, were popular for bouncing around

McDonald's, a fast-food restaurant, specializing in hamburgers, becomes a national franchise

1956 CREST becomes the first toothpaste to add fluoride to reduce cavities

1957 People with unkempt hair and beards, who listened to jazz, read poetry and used slang, were called Beatniks

13-year-old Bobby Fischer becomes chess champion

FRISBEES, colorful plastic saucers that are wisked though the air become a craze

1958 The *Cha Cha* is the new dance

HULA-HOOPS, wide, round colorful tubes, that twirl around the hips become a fad across America

1959 U.S. auto accident death toll over 1.25 million, more than in all U.S. wars combined

1959 Plastic YO-YO'S, controlled with a string for movement replaces the hula hoop as the latest fad

Mattel introduces the first BARBIE doll, a beautiful image of a real teenage girl

Fast Forwarding into the Fabulous Fifties ... the Best of Times

Introduction to the Decade

During the fifties, our nation was taking a leadership position in just about every area of life, at home and abroad. It was a decade in which science and technology lead the way. Color televisions, dishwashers, vacuum cleaners and refrigerators were the household appliances Americans wanted most. Prosperity was the buzz word and Americans were now focusing on establishing homes, building families and educating their children.

In 1948 Wayne Coy of the Federal Communications Commission was quoted as saying, "Make no mistake about it, television is here to stay." By the 1950's, he was proven to be right. Television, pictures transmitted into our living rooms, seen in black and white were replacing radio programs, in the homes of Americans, as the cost became affordable. By 1954 RCA had begun mass production of the first color television sets, but because of high costs associated with color broadcasting, it would be another 10 years before most families would be able to view programs in color.

Fran Toepfer and her family didn't mind, they were delighted to experience this new phenomena—being able to see as well as hear their favorite programs. In 1999, Fran, who was born and raised in upper Manhattan and has lived in Rockland County for over thirty years, fondly remembered how friends and neighbors would come to watch their new sensation, the T.V., short for television. A busy career woman, mother and homemaker, today Fran was active in her community and was writing as a poet, and entrepreneur. She brought her life experiences and insight to her poetry and other writings and found time to watch and remember, television "The Magic Box."

The Magic Box

Fran Toepfer

What excitement! I remember the talk in the neighborhood and the door to our apartment being left open so friends and neighbors could drop in—everyone wanting to see the Magic Box. We are one of the first families to have one and everyone wants to see it. What is this? Talking pictures? How can this be? Incredible!

The Magic Box is called television, TV for short. Television had few stations and very few shows, only in black and white. Wow! Have we come a long way in a few short years. Children's television of the fifties influenced our lives because the programs were created to keep children entertained while teaching valuable lessons. I remember Howdy Doody, the shows main character who was a freckled-faced puppet, wearing a western shirt, and kerchief, jeans, boots and gloves. He had big blue eyes and a huge smile. Clarabelle, the Clown, who never spoke a word, just squirted seltzer at other characters, was portrayed by Bob Keeshan, who would later become Captain Kangaroo. Howdy Doody kept a nation of children glued to the television set waiting for the host, Buffalo Bob to say, "Hey kids, what time is it?" They would all respond, "It's Howdy Doody Time!"

One of the earliest children's shows was Kukla, Fran and Ollie another puppet show. Burt Tillstrom, was the creator and voices for Kukla and Ollie. Fran stood speaking with them from outside their tiny stage. Kukla, meaning doll in Russian, was a bald, big-nosed puppet, while side kick, Ollie, short for Oliver J. Dragon, was a white toothed, lovable dragon.

Some of the other shows that came to the "little screen" were ventriloquist, Paul Winchell's Jerry Mahoney, with Kucklehead Smiff and

Romper Room. This was a popular show, as children from the audience participated in songs and games with the teachers who hosted the show.

The fifties also saw the beginning of some of the most popular and long running television shows. Captain Kangaroo, and Mr. Greenjeans entertained children with animals for years. The Mickey Mouse Club took off on the popularity of Mickey and started a club for children. Lassie was the story about a famous collie and her adventures with two families, first the Millers, then the Mortons. Rin-Tin-Tin, a German Shepard was another famous dog, who played side-kick to Rusty, a young orphan boy, befriended by a soldier; all living in Fort Apache. Superman and The Lone Ranger epitomized the heroes we all searched for in childhood.

Evening entertainment revolved around variety shows and comedy. Who could ever forget The Ed Sullivan Show? Sullivan, a New York columnist, brought a variety of talent to television, including Elvis Presley. Comedians Red Skelton and Milton Berle kept us laughing, while the Nelson Family, the Cleavers of "Leave It To Beaver" and the Andersons of "Father Knows Best" rounded out our family entertainment.

Two of my favorite entertainers were Les Paul and Mary Ford, whose music kept us entertained, while "The Hit Parade," kept us abreast of the most popular songs of the day. I always enjoyed music and loved to listen to the radio. Now, I actually could see the artist performing and was enjoying the experience.

Remembering those days when my friends would come over to watch the afternoon T.V. shows still brings a big smile to my face. It was such magic! We couldn't understand how it worked, but we were certainly glad it did.

Those were such carefree, fun times. We knew technology was on the move, but we never dreamed it was about to explode and charge forward, taking giant steps into the future. Today television delivers pictures to our living rooms, in blazing living color, not only from around the world, but from outer space. I still find this Magic Box, called television, amazing.

Introduction to the Story

Our soldiers came back home following World War II and the Korean War and families became the focal point of American life. Television was copying the scenario with shows like Father Knows Best, Leave It To Beaver and The Donna Reed Show.

These popular shows were idealistic portrayals of family life, but a child's real world of the fifties was often very different. Looking at that time through the eyes of an eight-year-old, our story is about one little girl, and her summer in the famous Catskill Mountains. Francine R. Cefola grew up to write many such stories and in 1999 turned that love of writing into The Write Source and Golden Quill Press. With over 25 years as a business writer and published author, she had written articles, short stories and poems, and her first novel, "Code 47 to B R E V Force." But, no matter how many adventures she wrote, she will always vividly remember the fifties; being eight and writing this story about going "Off to The Bungalow."

Off to the Bungalow

Francine R. Cefola

Summer vacation was about to begin. The three o'clock school bell sent me rushing to say my last goodbyes before racing the six city blocks home. The excitement I felt was magnified as I ran into my room and started gathering personal possessions I just knew I couldn't live without for the whole summer. I grabbed records, comic books, a deck of cards, a ball, jump-rope and as many games as I could get in the bag. That summer, June 1959, I was almost eight years old and with my favorite things going with me, I was looking forward to three fun-filled months without school in the country.

I hurried to get out of my school clothes and into my play clothes, while my mother combed my long hair into a rubber banded pony tail, just like hers. "Daddy wants to get going, so take your bags down to the car," she told me.

I dragged the stuffed bags out of the apartment and down three flights of marble steps to the front door. Holding the huge heavy door open with my foot, I barely squeezed through with the bags. I struggled down the remaining thirty high stoop steps; bags dragging behind me until I finally reached our car, a brown 1956 Oldsmobile 88. My brother was trying to help my father who was yelling about having more stuff to pack. Not wanting to get yelled at, I dropped the bags, turned and ran back up the steps to hurry my mother along.

After locking the apartment, my dog and I, with mother on our heels, dashed down the stairs. My father was already sitting impatiently in the car when my brother ran to open the front door for my mother. Finally, off we went.

The heat miraculously started to subside as soon as we reached the New Jersey side of the George Washington Bridge. Sitting in the back seat I was crunched between valises and my older brother, David. My dog Frisky, an all black, Welsh-Terrier-Pointer, with the cutest eyes, was squashed in with us. Moving around to get comfortable, I started to wonder about going from New York to New Jersey to get to the Catskill Mountains, which were in New York. But we had made this trip every year since 1951, so I guessed it must be right.

Already I was anxious to get to our first stop. Sometimes it would be "The Red Apple Rest," a roadside stop on Route 17, where you could get food and use the rest room. I always hoped no one had to go to the bathroom so we could keep going and stop at "The Three Bears" where I could fill up on the only thing they had—ice cream.

We were going to "Morris Cottages," a group of small connected houses called bungalows, with no heat and very small rooms, in upstate New York, just down the road from the famous Concord Hotel.

After the stops and the long ride I could finally see the sprawling white Concord buildings, proudly overlooking Kiamesha Lake. The Concord Hotel was famous for all of its lavish facilities. There was a world of things to do and many families would come there for vacations, but we were lucky enough to be there all summer. From our bungalow colony we could walk to the hotel and sneak in through unguarded areas. We always had to be on the lookout for the security guards, but once you were on the hotel grounds no one questioned if you belonged.

At night, men and women would dress in formal attire and parade through the hotel lobby on their way to a lavish cocktail hour before they entered one of the dining rooms for a delicious meal. The hotels in the Catskill Mountains were known for their extravagant food, serving three huge sit-down meals a day at which you could order as much food as you wanted.

After dinner, the guests would go into the ballroom and dance as the bands played the music of Frank Sinatra and other crooners. I liked to dance the Cha-Cha and fast Lindy. After dancing, came the evening's entertainment, a show with famous celebrities, such as Eddie Fisher, Lena Horne, Sammy Davis Jr., just to name a few.

As we rounded the bend, the hotel faded from sight and I knew, finally, we're here! Frisky jumped up and down and I know she knew it too. I saw the big, white Main House, the residence of the owners and the location of the main telephone and loud speaker system from which all announcements were made. I could almost hear the static of the microphone turning on, then two loud blows, and finally the long awaited announcement, for a telephone call, which had to be taken at a booth in the middle of the colony or to pick up mail at the Main House. I always liked, "Attention! Dugans or Bungalow Bar is on the premises." That meant the bakery man and ice cream truck had arrived. I would hurry and get money or I'd miss getting the best cupcakes and ice cream.

As we drove up the gravel road we passed the casino, where the Tuesday night movies, weekend dances and live entertainment were held. I really enjoyed the movies because I got to stay up late. My favorites were Danny Kaye's, "The Five Pennies," about a musician who gives up his career to help save his polio stricken child and Rosalind

Russell's "Auntie Mame," a women of extravagance and her love for her nephew. Also, Doris Day and Rock Hudson movies were terrific boy and girl love stories.

The casino was also a hang out for us kids. There was a coke bottle machine outside, while inside there were wooden "knock hockey boards" for two players who would use wooden sticks to knock a wooden puck into the opposing sides slot. I got a lot of splinters, but had fun. There were also two pin-ball machines. I was a champ because I knew how to shake the machines just enough so they didn't tilt.

I could now see the huge green lawn which divided the two rows of 54 bungalow units and turned my attention to our bungalow, # 2G. As my father parked the car in our space, I grabbed Frisky's leash and jumped out of the car. I waited impatiently while my mother came to open the lock. The inside of our bungalow was just as I had remembered. I looked around, letting Frisky sniff things out on her own. My mother started to unload packages while I inspected the rooms making sure all my things were still there. This had always been our bungalow, so we left our things there from one summer to the next. I sought out and found the ceramic ashtrays and lanyards I had made in camp and my treasured picture of singer, actor Fabian. Then I searched for my stack of classic comic books, Archie and Superman, including the 1958 anniversary issues. I was relieved they were all still there and in good condition; especially the anniversary issues which I collected because they contained so many great stories.

The front room of our bungalow was a combination kitchen, dining room, sitting room and bedroom. The kitchen table was red and white aluminum with four matching chairs. The hall area had a mirrored closet where I stopped to check how I looked before proceeding to the bathroom. I stuck my head in to be sure mom's favorite shower curtain was still hanging before I turned the small corner to the bedroom. The two twin size beds with wooden headboards were just as my mother had left them, plastic covering the mattresses and the smell of camphor which she had sprinkled around to keep the bugs away. The beds took up most of the room. We didn't have television, private telephones or heat for the cool summer country nights, but we never seemed to miss any of our city conveniences.

To keep me from being underfoot, my mother sent me out to walk Frisky while she cleaned and my father and brother finished unloading the car. We walked to the pool and I stood with my dog at my heels, watching the water flowing into the six foot deep end, while reminiscing about summers past.

The pool was the congregating area for the parents during the day. They played cards and Mah-Jongg, and listened to comedians like Jackie Mason, while the kids swam 'til they were almost blue, from the ice cold water. Looking beyond the pool, I could see the handball court and the baseball field where our day camp would challenge other colony camps in kickball, volleyball and baseball. I hated camp, except for the year end shows we put on. So maybe this year I would be able to convince my parents that, at almost eight years old, I was grown up enough not to have to go.

What a great summer I would have. I would hang out at the bowling alley with the older kids, watching the cute boys set up the pins, while playing my favorite songs on the juke box. Or I could go into town, to the candy store and play pool or pin ball and read comics and watch the guys. In my spare time I could go to other colonies and look for guys . . . but I know my parents, they'll make me go to camp.

Suddenly, I got a brilliant idea. If I wait until Sunday night when my father goes back to the city, I'll have a whole week before he comes back for the weekend to try and convince my mom. Then I heard her calling and I realized I had been gone for a long time. I had hoped to see some of my other friends who were also now arriving, but that would have to wait until later. As Frisky and I ran back across the lawn I stopped just short of the bungalow and bent down to give her a hug . . . and then I said a little prayer, "Please let this be a great summer and please don't let me be in trouble already."

Fast Forwarding into the Fabulous Fifties . . . the Best of Times   83

Introduction to the Story

The 1950's brought new ways of life that many older citizens had trouble understanding. The older generation felt what we had fought and died for, was good enough, while the members of the younger generation were looking to spread their wings and experience all the new possibilities on the horizon.

    The previous story gave us a glimpse of the fifties from a child's point of view. "That's How It Should Be," gives us a glimpse of how the older generation viewed the happening of those times. Authors, Marilyn Benkler and Ellen Ziegler were long time friends and colleagues and were inspired to write this story by a guest they had met while teaching art at a nursing home. In 1999, Marilyn Benkler was a singer, artist, actress and writer who enjoyed teaching fine art, voice and piano. She was also a published author and award winning sculptor. She performed in numerous shows and was the mother of three daughters and a very proud grandmother.

    In 1999, Ellen Ziegler was a professional artist and published writer who taught fine art and creative writing. She had published poetry, short stories and articles. Her song lyrics have won awards. She was a mother of two sons.

    "That's How It Should Be," was entered into "TELL IT TO THE FUTURE," a national writing contest, for writers whose stories typified experiences during different decades of the 1900's. This story won first prize. Golden Quill Press is pleased to present this Award Winning Story in its entirety.

That's How It Should Be

Marilyn Benkler and Ellen Ziegler

December 31, 1959

Dear Emma:

The sun is shining as I sit and write this letter to you. I've just finished picking out the seeds I want to plant in the flower box outside my window. I look forward to showering, getting dressed and waiting for the kids to come.

Tammy bought me a pink shirt for my birthday with her babysitting money. She said it's the kind you don't have to iron. I remember how you used to sing when you ironed. I'm not so sure about wearing the Mickey Mouse tie Dean gave me, but I don't want to hurt his feelings. He's going through a stage now where he wants to be a rock 'n' roll star. Do you remember when he was two and kept taking the pots and pans out of Pam's cabinet and banging them with a spoon? You said he'd be a drummer someday. Emma, he started a band in the garage of their new house and drives Pam and Harry crazy playing "Rock Around the Clock" over and over again. Tammy, who's as cute as can be, wanted to be the lea-d singer, but Dean said she was too square. She didn't like that, so she turned up the sound full blast on her hi-fi record player and drowned him out. You can't imagine the racket they make.

Tammy reminds me of you in that she won't let anyone take advantage of her. They're good kids, Emma, but it's been a tough decade to raise children. Just as we were recovering from World War II, the Korean War started and the new president, Truman, gave the order to build an H-bomb. It would have turned your world upside down to see where the country was heading.

The Russians blasted a rocket ship called "Sputnik" into space, then we sent up a rocket with two monkeys. The Soviet leader, Khrushchev, threatened to press a red button and blow us to smithereens. We had a red button, too.

It affected the children. Harry and Pam began talking about building a bomb shelter in their backyard. Tammy started putting her porcelain dolls back in their boxes at night. It almost broke my heart when she said, "Grandpa, the fallout could hurt them if I don't get them in the bomb shelter in time."

Dean pretended like it didn't bother him, but his nails were bitten down to the quick. I later found out that every time a special alarm bell rang at school, to signal a bomb drill, he and the other children had to duck under their desks, with their arms folded to protect their heads and eyes in case of shattering glass.

Things have calmed down a bit now. Dean is interested in girls and Tammy wants to be a singer like Patti Page. Pam's started her on piano and voice lessons.

I can almost hear you saying, "That's how it should be."

You'd be proud of me, Emma. I try to show the kids how to live their lives to the fullest, to make every minute count, and that people are more important than material things. In this day and age there are distractions and temptations you wouldn't believe. The kids watch too much television. They forget to talk to each other. On the weekend they spend their allowance in the new shopping center near their house. I know you would tell them it's more important that they learn who they are and how to help each other, than what they can invent or build or spend. Lord knows, Emma, all these new inventions would drive you crazy. Pam's got a central vacuum cleaning system in the house. I remember our old carpet sweeper and how you didn't want to give it up.

Harry just laid out $6,000 for a new Caddy so Pam can have the Chrysler to taxi the kids around. Did we teach him to spend money like that? Not that I recall. I thought we taught him to save. I know what you're thinking, "As long as he's healthy and happy let him do what he wants." He is happy. You'd be proud of him, too. He helped design a new computer called the UNIVAC and they used it during President Eisenhower's election.

Harry told me, "The computer will carry more information than one man's brain can handle," and I told him, "If the computer has all the information we might forget to think."

These inventions change as fast as new cars flying by on the highways. They're too much for me to keep up with.

There's no machine that can duplicate the human touch. I can't imagine there ever being one. You taught me that. When I wanted to buy you a sewing machine you said it wouldn't feel the same as hand-stitching the children's clothes. I thought you were making it hard on yourself, but I see now what you meant. Nothing can compare to the feeling of working with your hands.

Emma, I'm going to plant the seeds in the window box. The flowers will brighten up my room in the nursing home. When the children come I'll teach them how. I'm going to say goodbye for now.

Your loving husband,

Gerald

P.S. I miss you so much. These ten years have passed so slowly ... without you. The memory of your touch keeps me alive. And that's how it should be.

Conclusion of the Decade

The fifties saw the ending of the Korean war and the advances in assuring civil rights. Great progress was made in the fight against diseases and technology was moving our country forward. The fifties spawned many firsts that would change how we looked at the world. Credit cards, television with T.V. Dinners, fluoride toothpastes and a whole world of plastics became a part of our lives. But one of the biggest changes would be spawned from an unknown source. Rock 'n' roll changed how we looked at our youth. The younger generation had found its voice through their music. The older generation was adjusting to the changes that were occurring between the traditional ways of life and the newer more liberal attitudes. By the time we approached the sixties a whole new world was dawning, but little did we know where this new decade would take us?

We dedicate this chapter to all the men and women who served our country during the Korean War to protect our shores and safeguard our country's freedom.

1960's

7

A Time Of Love . . .
A Time Of Hate . . .
A Nation Rocked By Change

1960-1969

We were questioning our values and
where our country was going.

Memorable Events of the Decade

PRESIDENTS AND THEIR FIRST LADIES

1960–1961 34th Dwight D. Eisenhower First Lady Mary "Mamie" Geneva Dowd
1961–1963 35th John F. Kennedy First Lady Jacqueline Bouvier
1963–1969 36th Lyndon B. Johnson First Lady Claudia "Lady Bird" Taylor
1969 37th Richard M. Nixon First Lady Thelma "Pat" Ryan

MAJOR EVENTS OF THE UNITED STATES AND WORLD HISTORY

1960 Presidential debates are televised for the first time

The Soviets shoot down a U.S. Spy Plane piloted by Francis Gary Powers

1961 John F. Kennedy, 43, becomes the youngest, and the first Roman Catholic president

13 black and white "Freedom Riders" test racial segregation on buses that cross state lines

The Berlin Wall separates East and West Berlin into Communist and Free rule

1962 The Cuban Missile Crisis is a week-long threat of nuclear war from Soviet missiles in Cuba

1963 Nuclear Test Ban Treaty is signed by U.S., U.S.S.R., and Great Britain

200,000+ marchers, the largest civil rights demonstration in history gather in Washington

Dr. Martin Luther King, Jr., delivers his "I Have a Dream," speech at the Lincoln Memorial

President Kennedy is assassinated in Dallas, Texas

1964 Civil Rights Act bans discrimination for race, religion, sex or origin in public places and employment

Dr. Martin Luther King, Jr., wins The Nobel Peace Prize

The Palestinian Liberation Organization, (PLO), forms to fight Israel

Gulf of Tonkin resolution gives President Johnson the right to send troops without declaring war

American Troops land in Vietnam

1965 Thousands of Civil Rights demonstrators march from Selma to Montgomery Alabama

A Time Of Love . . . A Time Of Hate . . . A Nation Rocked By Change

The Voting Rights Act prevents states from using devices to prevent blacks from voting

Students protest the bombing of North Vietnam

President signs a bill creating Medicare—to assist senior citizens with medical costs

1967 Israel defeats Arab forces, Syria, Jordan and Egypt in the Six Day War

Egypt closes The Suez Canal

Thurgood Marshall becomes the first black Supreme Court Justice

1968 U.S. navy ship, *Pueblo* is captured in North Korea

Civil Rights Leader, Dr. Martin Luther King, Jr., is assassinated

Riots erupt in Chicago at the Democratic National Convention

Senator Robert Kennedy, brother of assassinated, President John F. Kennedy, is assassinated

First U.S. troops withdrawn from Vietnam

1969 Astronaut Neil Armstrong, is the first man to walk on the moon

IMPORTANT ADVANCES IN SCIENCE AND TECHNOLOGY

1960 First birth control pill approved for sale by the FDA, Food and Drug Administration

U.S. Nuclear Submarine, *Triton* circumnavigates the globe under water

American Heart Association attributes smoking to higher death rate

1961 Oral Polio vaccine in use

First Intercontinental Ballistic Missile (ICBM) fired

Russian cosmonaut, Yuri Gagarin, is the first man in space

Astronaut, Alan Shepard, makes the first U.S. space flight

1962 John Glenn becomes the first American to orbit the Earth

1964 Swedish photographer Lennart Nilsson's pictures reveal a living human embryo

The Verrazano-Narrows Bridge, Staten Island, New York, opens, becoming the World's Longest Suspension Bridge

IBM's word processor converts and stores typing

The U.S. Surgeon General warns the public of the hazards of smoking

1967 South African surgeon Dr. Christiaan Barnard performs the first human heart transplant

Dolby Sound is used to filter out background noise in recordings for better quality

1968 U.S. Explodes an experimental hydrogen bomb in Las Vegas

Robert Dennard patents RAM-Random Access Memory the basis for memory in computers

SPOTLIGHT ON THE WORLD OF ENTERTAINMENT

1960 *The Flintstones* about a stone-age family is the first prime time cartoon

Black Entrepreneur, Berry Gordy, starts Motown Records to promote black artists

Alfred Hitchcock's, classic movie *Psycho* terrifies audiences with its famous shower scene

1962 *Fail Safe* by E. Burdick and H. Wheller epitomizes the fears of nuclear war

$40 million *Cleopatra*, brings stars Elizabeth Taylor and Richard Burton, together on and off screen

Rachel Carson's *Silent Spring* starts the environmental protection movement

Adults catch on to rock 'n' roll and dance to Chubby Checker's song, *The Twist*

1963 Guggenheim Museum, New York City, pop-art show includes Andy Warhol's painting of a soup can

Betty Friedan's *The Feminine Mystique* starts the modern womens' rights movement

Joan Baez and Bob Dylan's folk music offer deep views of love and war

1964 British rock band, the *Beatles'* U.S. tour includes a performance on the *Ed Sullivan Show*

Peace, love, drugs and flower power—the creed of *Hippies* who *Turn On, Tune In, Drop Out*

The United Nations unveils Marc Chagall's tribute to former U.N. Secretary-General Dag Hammarskjold

1966 The new Metropolitan Opera House opens in New York's Lincoln Center

Star Trek, science fiction treatment of modern day problems begins on television

A Time Of Love . . . A Time Of Hate . . . A Nation Rocked By Change

135,000 gather in New York City's Central Park for an outdoor concert given by singer Barbra Streisand

1967 *The Graduate* epitomizes young people rejecting their parents standards and way of life

Hair, the first Broadway musical based on rock emphasizes the issues of war, drugs and free love

1968 Hard Rockers Jimi Hendrix and Janis Joplin's music compete with Aretha Franklin's soul sound

Rowan and Martin's Laugh-In's political humor and catchphrases characterize our countries unrest

2001: A Space Odyssey sets the stage for a revolution in special effects

1969 Nudity comes to Broadway when *Oh! Calcutta* opens

Over 300,000 attend Woodstock Music Festival for three days of free music, amid drugs and love-ins

Sesame Street bridges the gap between education and fun learning using advertising techniques

SPORTS' HIGHLIGHTS

1960 Pittsburgh Pirate, Bill Mazeroski hits the winning home run to beat the New York Yankees in the World Series

Arnold Palmer wins golf's U.S. Open

1961 Jack Nicklaus wins U.S. Golf Association Amateur

ABC premieres *Wide World of Sports*, television show totally devoted to sports

NFL commissioner Pete Rozelle lobbies Congress to legalize single-network television contracts

Roger Maris, New York Yankee outfielder hits 61 home runs, breaking Babe Ruth's record

1962 Sonny Liston defeats Floyd Patterson to become world heavyweight boxing champ

Basketball's Philadelphia Warriors' Wilt Chamberlain scores 100 points against the New York Knicks

1963 U.S. Tennis team wins the Davis Cup

1967 New York Yankees' outfielder Mickey Mantle hits his 500th home run

Billie Jean King becomes the top American and International woman tennis player

First football Super Bowl is won by the Green Bay Packers 35-10 over the Kansas City Chiefs

1968 Figure Skater, Peggy Fleming wins the only U.S. Gold Medal at the Winter Olympics

1969 UCLA's Lew Alcindor, considered one of the greatest college basketball players ever

New York Jets and Quarterback Joe Namath beat the favorite Baltimore Colts in Super Bowl III

Curt Flood files suit against the Commissioner of baseball and the owners over being traded

San Francisco Giant, Willie Mays hits his 600th home run

New York's "Miracle" Mets, underdogs in the World Series defeat the favored Baltimore Orioles

OTHER INTERESTING FACTS

1960 U.S. Population reaches over 179 million

Millions of televisions sets become common place in homes in the U.S.

Oral contraceptives are first used

16-year-old Bobbi Fischer wins the U.S. Chess Title

Aluminum cans are used for foods and beverages

1964 The Worlds Fair opens in New York

Permanent Press clothing makes ironing a thing of the past

1965 Soft Contact Lenses, give longer, more comfortable wear

The Miniskirt, a mid-thigh length skirt, becomes the latest fashion statement

1966 Color Television becomes popular

Author and activist, Betty Friedan, helps to found the National Organization for Women (NOW)

1968 Richard M. Nixon is elected President by the narrowest margin since 1912

1969 The Department of Defense sets up a network of computers and the Internet is born

A Time Of Love . . . A Time Of Hate . . . A Nation Rocked By Change

Introduction to the Decade

With television becoming a staple in American homes, more of the population was becoming better informed of events in our country and in the world. This portal also opened up a Pandora's box resulting in the youth of our nation questioning everything. The sixties started out as an idealistic time, characterized by our President and First Lady. The Kennedy's epitomized a time of family, elegance, education and community service. Jacqueline Bouvier Kennedy became a role model for women and young girls who followed her fashions and admired her personal accomplishments. President Kennedy's charisma, charm and easy going manner set a tone for Americans . . . until fear gripped our nation. The "Camelot" years were soon to end as one event led to another: the Cuban Missile Crises, President Kennedy's Assassination, War in Vietnam, struggle for Civil Rights, and the assassinations of Dr. Martin Luther King, Jr., and Robert Kennedy. Marches, protests, violence created a nation tearing itself apart.

    Anne M. Ogle captured her feelings about this era, in her poem, "Impressions—From the Sixties." She paints vivid pictures of the roller coaster changes and challenges of this turbulent time. In 1999, Anne lived in Oregon, where she was working on her second novel. When she was not writing poetry or short stories, she spent time with her cat. Her poetry has been published in *The Poets Hand* and *the American Poetry Annual*.

Impressions— From the Sixties

Anne M. Ogle

COMMITMENT
OPTIMISM
DISENCHANTMENT

GRADUATION
HATS AND TASSELS THROWN HIGH
IN THE DISTANT THE THUNDER CRIES

BEACH
    LYING IN THE SUN
          DREAMING

A RIDERLESS HORSE
PRANCES
ONE NOVEMBER MORN

BLACK MAN
WITH A DREAM
NOW HE IS GONE

BURNING CROSSES
    WHITE HOODED FIGURES
        ANGRY BLACK FACES

i looked across the sea
on the other side vietnam
on this side me

a man and woman
exchanging rings
not knowing what the future brings

children banging
on xylophones
children eating ice cream cones

full of guilt
a friend dies in vietnam
and here i am

candlelight vigil
riot
flag burning

velvet jackets
gypsy style skirts
funky look

drugs and drink
forget the pain
forget the joys

apollo eleven on tranquility sea
one giant step for mankind
one giant step for me.

Introduction to the Story

Robert Reeg was born and raised in New York City where he graduated high school from Power Memorial Academy, and attended Iona College. Later he received his Paramedic certification from Albert Einstein College of Medicine, and served five years as a Paramedic throughout New York City. Robert's story gives us a glimpse into some of his boyhood experiences that are amusing as well as vivid impressions of the times. This poignant tale will take you on this young man's journey; leading the reader to understand the man who grew up to be appointed to the New York City Fire Department in 1982, as a member of Engine Company 44. In 1999 Robert was promoted to Fire Marshal, as an arson investigator, assigned to the Bureau of Fire Investigation's, Manhattan base, and resided with his wife Marie and daughters Alison and Erin, in Stony Point, New York.

Reflections: On Where Have All the Flowers Gone?

Robert Reeg

The chorus of, "Hell No, We Won't Go" echoed off the walls of the ancient brick building that lined Amsterdam Ave in New York City. Our Dean of Discipline, Brother Binkley, stood atop the weather beaten steps, glaring down at us. Then sounding very much like a Marine

A Time Of Love . . . A Time Of Hate . . . A Nation Rocked By Change

Corps Drill Instructor he bellowed, "One more time and you will all have detention for a month." Silence instantly ensued, and our group of musicians quietly boarded the "paddy wagons." No, it wasn't a war protest, but the band members of Power Memorial Academy being transported to city hall. Our band was to play at a memorial service for a couple of cops who had been gunned down by a group of militant black radicals known as the, "Black Panthers." To save Power Memorial the expense of hiring buses, the New York City Police Department had provided these seedy vehicles, which were usually reserved for transporting criminals to prison. Our chant, "Hell No, We Won't Go!" was merely in jest; catholic school boys rebelling.

While performing at memorial services was nothing new, the death of a cop, or a comrade for that matter, was a foreign concept to us. Despite the "Grim Reaper's" presence all around us, we possessed a feeling of invulnerability; death was something we had yet to fully grasp.

The media was exerting a diligent effort to sway public opinion concerning the Vietnam War. Televised images of disgruntled G.I.'s tossing bloated, oozing body bags aboard muddy, blood stained helicopters were beginning to have the desired effect. The anti-war movement was gathering momentum, and dissension over the war seemed to be tearing our country apart. I recall announcements being made over the classroom loudspeaker, "we regret to announce the death of 'So and So' class of '65, who died in the service of his country." Even as the deaths of "Power" alumni became more frequent, death itself however, remained something intangible to us—lingering on the fringe of our consciousness.

En route to the service we all took turns at demonstrating our musical talents. Jimmy's incredible trumpet rendition of "Summertime," a hit from the musical Porgy and Bess, was as sweet as if the famous vocalist Paul Robeson sat there serenading us. Standing on the steps of city hall, Jimmy's moving interpretation of taps brought tears to our eyes. About a year later Jimmy's trumpet was silenced forever, when his chopper crashed in the La Drang Valley, Republic of Vietnam. It was only after we played at Jimmy's memorial service that the idea occurred to the rest of us, "Hey, we could be next!"

Perhaps this is a rueful manner to begin a story of the sixties, but that's the way I remember it. It was a decade of change, a time of conflict. A period when our nation endured unbearable sorrow, and relished in indescribable joy. There was John F. Kennedy's inspirational inaugural address and years later, his small son John-John saluting his coffin. There was the incinerated Apollo tomb; there was Neil Armstrong on the moon. There were a dozen fireman buried in a building collapse and the foundation laid for the World Trade Center. There were political assassinations; there was the flamboyant quarterback of the New York Jets, Joe Namath, with his index finger held high in triumph. There was the Democratic Convention in Chicago, there were the miracle New York Mets, World Series Champions.

Later as I sat enjoying the jam session aboard the "paddy wagon," I noticed a collage of graffiti on the prisoner's bench in front of me. This collection of graffiti was like a Rosetta Stone inscribed with all the hatred and hope of the times. Scratched into the ubiquitous peace symbol which held center stage, was another slogan of the day, "bomb Hanoi." Accompanying this absurdity were words of wisdom on just about every topic of the day; racial tensions, sex, sports, drugs, and music. It was like peering into a sorcerer's boiling caldron of strife.

I was astounded by the irony of the situation as I read all the kudos dedicated to the Black Panthers. Here we were, a group of mostly white boys, performing at a memorial for a black Police Officer, who was murdered by the Black Panthers. It just didn't make sense.

I grew up in a pretty strict household. Teenage years between fathers and sons have always been challenging, but the sixties must have been even more so. Drug wars were being fought on city streets, and soldiers were coming home from war strung out on heroin. My brother was in Vietnam, and I attended high school in "Hell's Kitchen," in New York City, an economically depressed area known for hoodlums and gang wars. No wonder my father always looked worried!

Another phenomenon of the sixties was the introduction of oral contraceptives. This new found freedom changed society's sexual mores in short order. I still recall my father's "pendulum" lecture.

"Robby" he emphatically stated, "all this sexual promiscuity will cause the 'morals pendulum' to swing the other way. It will swing back to Puritanism, because a new plague will be unleashed upon humanity."

I used to think that he was nuts. Today the ardor of a young couple's first embrace is tempered by fear of contracting sexually transmitted diseases, (at least that's what I hear). Apparently my old man knew what he was talking about! As this is a "G" rated article, that's all I have to say about that.

Today I listen to the same kinds of music my kids do. In the sixties my parents went from listening to fox trots and Frank Sinatra, to the Beatles and hard rock guitarist, Jimi Hendrix. It must have been excruciating.

The last aphorisms that I recall being scratched on the bench were a few phrases that you don't hear young people speak about today; "do your own thing, and question authority." I think above all, the idea of individuality was key in the sixties. Back then our nations' campuses never would have tolerated the political correctness of today. If I remember correctly, dissension was in fact, encouraged. Nowadays if you disagree with government policies, they label you as an extremist, or part of a conspiracy. What happened?

As I look back on those "good old days," the three events that stand out the most in my mind are; Kennedy's death, Neil Armstrong setting foot on the moon, and the New York Mets left fielder, Cleon Jones squeezing the last out of the 1969 World Series. As we humans dislike pain, we tend to remember past events more fondly than they actually occurred. To this day my father claims that his years in the service, were the best of his life; he "hit the beach" on Normandy during World War II!

Except for his fleshy lips and those gigantic crimson cheeks, I can't even remember what Jimmy the trumpeter looked like. I do however, think of him every time I hear that wonderful melody, "Summertime."

I wasn't the most accomplished saxophonist in the band. When my turn came, in the paddy wagon that day, to entertain the troops, I chose a simple tune that I had memorized. I vividly recall my pensive solo being rudely interrupted when our resident comedian blurted out, "Hey Reeg, ya wanna know where all the flowers went? Yule Gibbons (the original health food guru) ate them!"

Introduction to the Story

The lives of Naomi G. Anthony and millions of Americans were changed in the sixties by Dr. Martin Luther King, Jr.'s courageous fight against injustice. Naomi acknowledges that because of Dr. King's efforts, she has been able to bring her talents as an educator, singer, writer, story teller and a painter to a broader audience. She often teams with her husband, John who has appeared with the Metropolitan Opera. In 1999, they lived in West Nyack New York. Naomi has written a poignant story of how she felt upon hearing of the assassination of Dr. King and how his words have continued to be an inspiration. She says, "Born into a system of prejudice in the state of North Carolina, and spending my growing-up years in the south, gave me a deep appreciation for the Freedom Movement and its value to all American citizens."

Reflections on the Assassination of Dr. Martin Luther King, Jr.

Naomi G. Anthony

We heard the phone ringing as we approached the door of our apartment on the third floor of the New City, New York, Garden Apartments. My children, Jayon and Arthur, and I were returning from a fun-filled afternoon with a friend and her children. Our daughters, were nearly the same age, and our sons close in age. I hurriedly unlocked the door, rushed in and grabbed the phone. It was my husband, John; luckily he had not hung up. He was calling from New York City, where he had been on business since mid-morning of that beautiful spring day. He told me he'd let the phone ring a long time, hoping I'd pick it up.

"Where have you been?"

After I told him, he asked, "Have you heard the bad news?"

"What bad news?"

He replied, "Well, what we both thought might happen to Martin Luther King, has." His voice breaking.

"Oh no, don't tell me he's dead."

"He's been shot. It sounds serious. I'm on my way home, and I'll be there as soon as I can. Bye."

Speechless, I hung up the phone. Jayon, almost nine years old, noticed tears welling up in my eyes, "Mama, Mama, what's wrong? What's wrong? Why are you crying? Did something happen to Daddy?"

"No, Daddy's okay. He's on his way home."

Arthur, who was only six, was waiting anxiously to find out why I was upset. "Well, what's wrong then Mommy?"

I then repeated the sad message I received from their Daddy; "Martin Luther King has been shot. Let's turn on the TV." They responded to the news with shocked disbelief on their young faces. Reporters were announcing details of the assassination. It appeared everyone was stunned and bewildered.

Before John arrived home, we'd heard a television reporter announce that Dr. Martin Luther King, Jr., was dead. Following my initial feelings of devastation and horror over what had happened, I remember thinking, "Oh no! Now I'll never get a chance to join one of the civil rights demonstrations, and march with him."

When John arrived home, we rushed to him and we held on to each other, embracing and consoling one another. We sat talking about our country, and how our country had been blessed and made better by the work of this great man. As an American family we had witnessed Martin Luther King giving his all and sacrificing his life for an America he loved. He loved so much that he went to Rosa Parks' aid when she refused to move to the back of the bus and was taken off to jail. He organized the non-violent civil rights movement to change the "bad" bus law, and all other laws that had held the black people down so long, taking away their rights as human beings.

In his last speech, in Memphis, Dr. King said, "Let us stand with a greater determination. And let us move on in these powerful days, these days of challenge, to make America what it ought to be. We have an opportunity to make America a better nation."

The assassination of Dr. King left us feeling very sad, extremely upset, angry and depressed. The mixed emotions flooding my mind and heart did not last long. My mind became filled with thoughts of the monumental accomplishments of this great man. When I thought of all the positive changes his leadership had brought about, my spirit lifted with the realization he had brought a drastic change for the better and it would be mine to experience. I could finally do so many things I'd longed to do. I'd be able to enter places black people had been denied entrance to for so long. Finally, my civil rights had been achieved. I felt joyous that our two young children could now grow up in the country of their birth with their civil rights protected. They would not have to suffer the segregated practices I had endured during my childhood. Realizing this, helped me to focus on Dr. King's life, rather than his untimely death.

I admired that brave act of Rosa Parks, the spark of the freedom movement, which spurred the 1955 year long Montgomery bus boycott. Black people had suffered immeasurably in our country because of the rampant injustices of unconstitutional segregation laws. But now, thank God, we could face the future with courage, believing the words of the battle hymn of the civil rights movement's song of hope, "We Shall Overcome."

I was thirty-three years old on that bleak day in 1968 when Dr. Martin Luther King, Jr., was shot and killed. On that day I thought about how educationally handicapped I'd been for so many years. The teachers, who were colored, as they were called then, did the best they could in the three room weather-beaten, unpainted wooden-framed, elementary school I attended, from age seven through eleven. They taught using the hand-me-down worn-out books, furniture and other teaching tools and materials. We walked to school having to pass by a beautiful large red brick school—for the white children only. Their lush green playground and lovely school grounds put our "all dirt" schoolyard to shame; the shame was not on us, but on the southern whites who were in charge. I found myself smiling as I realized I would finally be allowed to enter a public library in the South. I could swim in the Atlantic Ocean and enjoy the beach whenever I pleased. I'd be free to drink from any water fountain, use a public restroom, ride sitting in the seat of my choice on the buses, and any public form of transportation and not be forced to move or leave. I could go to the school of my choice and send my children to schools and any public educational facility of our choice. Public parks no longer segregated, now would be open to us to enjoy. Churches previously closed to black people, would no longer be off limits to them. That hypocritical practice had always struck me as anti-Christian. I found my smile broadening, thinking about the fact that the signs, "Negro or Colored" and "White or Whites Only," would be taken down and most assuredly destroyed.

One regret permeating my mind was that I had never gotten the chance to march in a civil rights demonstration with Dr. King. After expressing this feeling to my understanding husband, we decided we'd go to Dr. King's funeral down in Atlanta, on that sad day of April 9, 1968.

We went, and we marched with the throngs of people in the miles long procession to the grave site. It was an extremely hot day. I thought I had worn shoes that would be comfortable to walk in, however, due to the extremely hot pavement, my feet began to feel miserable. There was no way to relieve the growing discomfort; the streets were just too hot for bare feet. I walked the long distance in pain. This pain I embraced feeling my suffering was for his sake, and knowing that because he had suffered, my life would hereafter be better. My pain also made me realize more fully, the untold misery many other marchers must have endured, while taking part in the numerous non-violent demonstrations of the civil rights movement. As we marched, I thought how so many Americans, especially those who had suffered oppression, would now have their civil rights protected. While walking on my raw, swollen and burning feet, I thought of the old freedom song, "I ain't gonna let nobody turn me around. I'm gonna keep on a walkin', keep on a talkin', marchin' up to freedom land."

CONCLUSION OF THE DECADE

The sixties were a pivotal time. The decade brought about change in how people viewed daily life. Civil rights changed how we related to our neighbors and our youth took on a new role, getting the vote at eighteen and rapidly changing many of the more stoic customs of the past. Dress, music, manners and morals all changed. Ways of doing business were less stringent leading to women taking a more dominant role in the workplace and as business owners. When the birth control pill was approved it added to the changing roles and moral concerns of our nation. Women felt freer to pursue careers and wait to be mothers, while having babies out of wed-lock became less of an issue. Even the music reflected this new age of freedom and questioning. The nation's young people were searching for ideals and modes of expression. Many chose to become "Hippies," questioning the values of the "Establishment," the government and their parents, while advocating, peace, love and sharing. The older generation, shook their heads and held their breath waiting to see where this generation was going. We began to believe that healing would come, as our troops were being withdrawn from Vietnam and we proudly rejoiced in an American's walk on the moon. The new decade would dawn with challenges to be met and a hope for our country's wholeness to be once again achieved.

1970's

8

From Crisis To Calm and Back Again . . . Where Do We Go From Here?

1970-1979

Trouble at home, trouble abroad . . .
amidst the celebration of our hundred years.

Memorable Events of the Decade

PRESIDENTS AND THEIR FIRST LADIES

1970 – 1974 37th   Richard M. Nixon   First Lady Thelma "Pat" Ryan
1974 – 1977 38th   Gerald R. Ford   First Lady Elizabeth "Betty" Bloomer
1977 – 1979 39th   James E. Carter   First Lady Rosalynn Smith

MAJOR EVENTS OF THE UNITED STATES AND WORLD HISTORY

1970 National Guard kills four Kent State University students who are protesting the Vietnam War

1971 Vietnam air strikes escalate

The "Pentagon Papers," reveal inconsistencies in government reports about the Vietnam War

Supreme Court rules that busing of students may be ordered to achieve racial desegregation

26th Amendment gives 18-year-olds the right to vote

President Nixon issues a 90 day freeze on wages and prices to curb inflation

1972 Five men arrested breaking into the Democratic Party National Headquarters in the Watergate

Gas shortage begins the "Oil Crisis"

Palestinian terrorists kill 11 Israeli athletes at the Munich Olympics

1973 Senate Watergate Committee hears White House officials testimony of President Nixon's involvement

Vice President Spiro Agnew resigns, after charges of bribes and income tax invasion while governor of Maryland

President Nixon chooses Gerald R. Ford as Vice President in accordance with the 25th Amendment

The Supreme Court case Roe v. Wade legalizes rights to an abortion

Arab nations attack Israel on its high holiday, Yom Kippur, but are swiftly defeated

U.S. troops officially leave Vietnam

1974 India becomes the sixth nation to explode a nuclear device

Richard M. Nixon resigns as President of the United States of America

From Crisis To Calm and Back Again . . .

President Ford pardons former President Nixon for any wrong doing while in office

1975 Unemployment reaches highest figures since 1941

1976 United States celebrates its Bicentennial—1776–1976

1977 President Carter grants a pardon to Vietnam War draft evaders

Egyptian President Anwar Sadat and Israeli leader Menachem Begin meet to discuss peace

1979 Americans at the U.S. Embassy in Iran are taken hostage

Soviets invade Afghanistan

IMPORTANT ADVANCES IN SCIENCE AND TECHNOLOGY

1970 Apollo 13 launched

First complete synthesis of a gene by scientists at the University of Wisconsin

Nobel Prize winner, Linus Pauling endorses the use of large doses of Vitamin C to prevent colds

1971 Discovery of two new galaxies next to the Milky Way

Intel produces the first commercial microprocessor, an integrated circuit for computers

The first pocket-calculator is produced by Texas Instruments

1972 CD's, Compact Discs on which music or data are recorded make their U.S. debut

CAT Scans, (computerized axial tomography), give enhanced images of the internal body

1973 NASA launches the first *Skylab,* an orbiting space station

Motorola debuts its hand-held cellular phone making calling possible from anywhere by anyone

1974 *Skylab* astronauts spend a record 84 days in space

Xerox develops the first computer with a "mouse," a hand-held devise that you point and click

Jay Heimlich announces his Heimlich Maneuver, a technique to save choking victims

1976 Reports indicate fluorocarbons, gases from spray cans cause damage to the earth's ozone layer

Viking 1 lands on Mars and begins transmitting the first photographs of another planets surface

Multiple Sclerosis, a nerve disease, is discovered to have viral cause

The supersonic transport (SST) *Concorde* first passenger jet to break the sound barrier

1977 First manned flight of U.S. Space Shuttle *Enterprise*

Uranus is discovered to have rings like Saturn—Spacecraft launched to probe Venus

Apple II, becomes the first mass market PC, (personal computer)

MRI scanner, (Magnetic Resonance Imaging), takes pictures of the internal body without X-rays

1978 Louise Brown the first "test-tube" baby conceived, is born in Great Britain

1979 Three Mile Island in Pennsylvania is the site of a nuclear power plant accident

SPOTLIGHT ON THE WORLD OF ENTERTAINMENT

1970 The singing group, the *Beatles,* John, Paul, George and Ringo break-up

All in the Family, TV sitcom, (situation comedy) creates Archie Bunker who dislikes everyone

1971 *Conceptual art,* concerned with making statements, becomes the craze

1972 Established actor, Marlon Brando stars in the sexually explicit *Last Tango in Paris*

1974 Journalists Woodward and Bernstein's *All The Presidents Men* chronicle the Watergate scandal

1975 Couples dancing *The Hustle* make the dance scene

Musicians strike closes 12 Broadway shows for 25 days

Saturday Night Live, late night comedy entertainment targets the famous and the not-so-famous

The Rocky Horror Picture Show, spoofing old time movies, gathers a cult following

1976 *One Flew Over the Cuckoo's Nest,* about a sane man in an insane world takes five top Oscars

Punk Rock, loud sounds with anarchic themes like *Sex Pistols' Anarchy in the U.K.,* begins

From Crisis To Calm and Back Again . . .

1977 *Roots*: Alex Haley portrays his family from slavery to modern times in a 12 hour T.V. mini-series

George Lucas' *Star Wars* sets new standards for sci-fi and visual effects—a box office sensation

1978 Vietnam movies, *Coming Home* and *The Deer Hunter* portray the horrors of the war

John Travolta's dancing to The Bee Gees songs in *Saturday Night Fever* begin the disco craze

1979 African-American Toni Morrison wins the National Book Award for *The Bluest Eyes*

Tom Wolfe's *The Right Stuff*, proudly depicts America's first astronauts

Apocalypse Now, dramatizes the realities of the Vietnam War

SPORTS' HIGHLIGHTS

1970 *Monday Night Football,* bringing fans a weekly game, other than on Sunday, debuts

1971 Boxer Joe Frazier defeats heavyweight champ Muhammad Ali

1972 U.S.'s Mark Spitz swims his way to seven gold medals at the Munich Olympics

"The Immaculate Reception"—deflected pass caught by Pittsburgh Steeler Franco Harris wins A.F.C. Playoff game

1973 *Secretariat* wins horse-racing Triple Crown

O.J. Simpson, football halfback, rushes for 2003 yards, to a one-year record

1974 Boxer Muhammad Ali defeats Joe Frazier, then beats George Foreman to regain the world title

Atlanta Braves, Hank Aaron, left-fielder, surpasses Babe Ruth's home run record of 714

1975 Billie Jean King wins her sixth Wimbledon Championship

Jack Nicklaus wins his fifth Masters and fourth Professional Golfers' Association Championship

Arthur Ashe becomes the first black national tennis player

1976 Romania's, Nadia Comaneci, records the first perfect score, a 10, on the uneven bars at the Olympics

1977 Gordie Howe makes hockey history with a total 1,000 professional career goals

1979 College basketball's Magic Johnson and Larry Bird go head to head for NCAA title

---
OTHER INTERESTING FACTS

1970 U.S. Population, 205 Million

1971 Cigarette advertisements banned from U.S. Television

"Hot Pants," micro-shorts become popular and acceptable as women's business attire

1972 President Nixon reelected in a landslide

Bobby Fischer wins the world chess title

PONG, an electronic version of ping-pong, (table tennis), is the world's first video game

The World Trade Center, 110 story twin tower, becomes the tallest building in the world

The Dow-Jones Industrial Average hits a record breaking "1,000" mark

The military draft is ended making the armed services all-volunteer

1973 "Skyjacking," terrorists kidnaping airplanes and passengers is a growing concern

Chicago's Sears Tower becomes the tallest building in the world

1974 President Ford becomes the only Vice President and President never elected to those offices

National speed limit of 55 miles per hour is established to conserve gasoline

Daylight Saving Time; changing time forward and backward, to save energy, is started in the U.S.

POST-IT NOTES, papers with stick, remove and re-stick capabilities come into use

Bar codes, computer scanned binary signal codes for identification, show up on more products

Unemployment reaches 9.2%

1975 U.S. and Soviet spacecrafts link 140 miles above the earth

Sony introduces BETAMAX, a home videocassette recording system (VCR)

Bill Gates and Paul Allen start Microsoft, to develop software for computers

- **1976** CB's, citizen band radio to talk to truckers and other drivers using "handles," (code names) are used
- **1977** New York City electrical failure, black-outs over nine million customers
- **1978** Polish Cardinal Wojtyla, becomes John Paul II, the first non-Italian Pope in over 450 years

    Auctioned *Gutenberg Bible* gets over $2 million, highest price ever paid for printed book
- **1979** Sony introduces the WALKMAN, a small portable tape player, with head-phones

    Suffragette, Susan B. Anthony becomes the first women honored on a U.S. coin

Introduction to the Decade

Much to our dismay, the country's unrest of the sixties continued as the seventies got off to a turbulent start. The nation was shocked and torn as the fighting in Vietnam continued. The war took center stage on our own streets and campuses and came blasting into our living rooms every night. President Nixon had been reelected in a landslide of confidence, only to have the country torn apart again by the Watergate scandal. Two years later the President would resign. Amid all this internal and external crisis, the country was dealing with high unemployment and then was hit with an oil crisis which caused substantial gas shortages. In spite of the downside, we were moving ahead in technology, with great strides in space and in the world of computers. Americans began to turn their hopes toward our country's Bicentennial and the promise of what the future could bring.

In true American spirit we continued to lead our lives and help our children to deal with the times. Such is the story of young Theresa Zarrella and her family. Theresa who was a teenager in the seventies, in 1999; is married, living in Rockland County, New York, with a family of her own. She did all the "cool teen things," of the seventies while keeping her serious desire to be a writer alive. She had started writing as a young child and was happy to see those dreams becoming reality. She was working on a novel for children, Theresa still sees life as she did years ago, as an adventure on "America's Golden Road."

On America's Golden Road

Theresa Zarrella

I snuggled up on the couch, to watch T.V. when a commercial came on about Walt Disney World, in Orlando Florida, a place with shows, rides, characters and so much to delight kids of all ages. That commercial conjured up wonderful memories of my first trip to that magical place when half the fun was just getting there.

It was the summer of 1978 and I was thirteen years old. My family had decided to take a two week vacation on the open American road, with Walt Disney World our destination. My father just loved our newly purchased red Ford Fairmont, and why not? With about 25 miles to the gallon, it would surely pave the way for cars of the future to become more gas efficient. After all, the oil crisis was still fresh in our minds and big gas guzzlers would eventually be on their way out.

We packed that car trunk as tightly as we could, making sure to leave room for souvenirs. Father made sure we had plenty of cold hard cash too, because he didn't trust credit cards. He thought they would just go the way of all those big gas guzzlers.

Our journey to Walt Disney World would take three days and my brother and I looked forward to taking turns sitting in the front seat with our father. There was much to see and so many places to explore. We were like little kids let loose in a toy store.

After a quick family prayer, a turn of the key and father's official "Yahoo," it was time to hit the road!

So off we went a happy traveling band of Disney crazed out fans. "America's Golden Road," Route I-95 would take us from New York to Florida; to the land of happiness and fun, in our case, Walt Disney World. As we drove along, I gazed out the window taking it all in, my senses on happy overload! We passed beautiful green trees of varied shapes and sizes, lakes, ponds and so much more. And oh, those billboards—those doggone billboards. My father said I-95 surely would go down in history for having the most billboards. There were billboards for the growing housing boom, advertising new home sites that were popping up everywhere like weeds. There were billboards for those new Polaroid cameras that could have your picture taken in 60 seconds and some for those new games that could be played right on your own T.V.! There were billboards for designer jeans and everything from tube socks to Star Wars movie stuff. It was like going through the yellow pages, except your car was doing the walking and not your fingers.

Halfway to Walt Disney World, Mother Nature was starting to brew up quite a heat wave, but our thirsty gang of die-hard Disney lovers, kept on trekking in our new red Ford Fairmont. Nothing could stop us. Not wild horses, nor bulldozers, well, nothing but "Stuckey's." After all those billboards and all those trees and ponds, thank goodness there was "Stuckey's." "Stuckey's" was the early version of the mega rest stops, only much smaller. We could get good fast food, eat at picnic tables and kids could play in the arcade, a place full of games of chance and skill. It had everything a convenience store would stock and very clean rest rooms. After filling our tummies with good food and then waiting in a long line of cars to get gas, away we went further south to the next friendly "Stuckey's." We were without a doubt, their best customers.

"America's Golden Road" was indeed wonderful. On long stretches where it seemed we were the only people on earth, our time was preoccupied with our "Silly Putty," a reusable, pliable rubber-like substance which could be molded into various fun shapes. We also enjoyed reading "Archie comics," "Mad magazines" and doing all the things teens do. After all it was a more than a thousand miles from home to Walt Disney World.

Father and Mother kept the radio tuned to their favorite stations. Frank Sinatra was father's all time favorite, while Neil Diamond, John Denver and bands playing romantic music were mother's favorites. Sometimes when father would sneak on the opera music, it was like being at Lincoln Center. You could hear him singing-a-long from New

York to Florida. When it got too loud, mother would be quick to shut the radio off. I'd ask her to turn it back on, happy that she couldn't get away from disco music; it ruled the airwaves. My brother and I loved bands like The Bee Gees, Abba and the Village People who were very popular at that time. Some of the songs I remember singing on that trip were from the disco movie "Saturday Night Fever," starring John Travolta.

With all the singing from the backseat, father started to search for other stations to check up on what was going on in the world. I remember hearing the news about the first test-tube baby, Louise Brown, who had been born in London and something about preparations being made for future Mid-East peace talks. The rest of the news was murders and killings, so I tuned it out. But my mind flashed to other news of the seventies. I remember hearing my parents talk about how bad those beginning years were. The long years of the Vietnam War and the protests that led to the killings at Kent State University in Ohio. Their voices reflected how scared they were that our country was being torn apart and how happy they were when the war finally ended and our soldiers came home. I was glad I was only five then and didn't know what was going on. But I did slightly remember the issue of "Watergate," the break-in at the Democratic National Headquarters by members of the Committee to Re-elect the President. My parents discussed the hearings and President Nixon's involvement. I remembered not understanding it, but being scared until it finally ended in 1974 when President Nixon resigned and President Ford granted him a pardon from prosecution for obstruction of justice. Those scarey years did produce one really good thing; the 26th. Amendment to the Constitution which gave 18-year-old's the right to vote—in five years that would be me. But on that day in 1978 I was just happy to be on my way to Walt Disney World, with my family, and all those bad times behind us. I guess Mom and Dad were thinking that too, because the radio dial quickly found its way back to the nearest music station.

After a long three days: 50 hamburgers, 15 hot dogs, 200 liters of Coke, a zillion billboards, 10 dozen Archie comics, 20 "Stuckey's" and one abused radio dial in need of replacing, we finally arrived at Walt Disney World! Overwhelmed with reaching our destination at long last, we all shouted out our loudest, Yahoo! I'm sure it could have qualified for the "Guinness Book of World Records," which kept track of such phenomena.

As I look back on my teen years, in the terrific seventies, I still remember that awesome magical place called Walt Disney World; it is paradise on earth to me and a place I believe everyone should see. I also remember looking forward to new experiences, like trekking back home to New York, on Route I-95, "America's Golden Road!"

Conclusion of the Decade

Americans breathed a sigh of relief as the seventies came to a close. The decade had finally taken an upward turn and the horrors that tore our country apart were starting to mend. The economy and world relationships were beginning to improve. Technology was moving ahead at a rapid pace changing the way we would be doing business and even the way we lived. Computers were coming into our homes and new inventions let us carry our music wherever we went and record our favorite television shows when we weren't home. We were once again safe, at home and abroad and had a positive feeling as we moved into the eighties. We faced the challenges our new advances were bringing, with confidence. We could not know that new and different problems would soon begin to loom on the horizon.

We dedicate this chapter to all the men and women who served our country during the Vietnam War to protect our shores and safeguard our country's freedom.

1980's

9

A Click of the Mouse...
a Zoom into Space...
Stock Market Up...
Stock Market Down

1980-1989

*The world and the economy sat
on the see-saw ... but technology
was surging us ahead.*

Memorable Events of the Decade

PRESIDENTS AND THEIR FIRST LADIES

1980 – 1981 39th James E. Carter   First Lady Rosalynn Smith
1981 – 1989 40th Ronald Reagan   First Lady Nancy Davis
1989   41st George Bush   First Lady Barbara Pierce

MAJOR EVENTS OF THE UNITED STATES AND WORLD HISTORY

1980 Lech Walesa leads a strike culminating in "Solidarity," Poland's first independent trade union

Due to the good economy the stock market begins its climb

Iraq launches an attack on Iran, starting a war

1981 Iran agrees to release the American hostages it had held captive for 444 days

U.S. air-traffic controllers strike

Assassination attempt on President Reagan by John Hinckley Jr.

British troops attack Argentina after the Argentinians invade the Falkland Islands

The Vietnam War Memorial, designed by Yale student Maya Yang Lin, is erected

1982 American Telephone and Telegraph, deemed a monopoly, is broken up into 22 local companies

1983 President Reagan announces "Star Wars," a plan for the defense against nuclear attack

President Reagan uses concerns for Americans in Grenada as a reason for a U.S. attack

1984 Geraldine Ferraro, becomes the first female Vice Presidential major party candidate

1985 The U.S. national debt is higher than amounts owed to us

Soviet leader, Mikhail Gorbachev, develops "Perestroika," restructure of the Soviet system

1987 Iran-Contra reveals profits from Iranian arms sales bought weapons for the Nicaraguan Contras

"Black Monday" as the Dow Jones plummets 508 points—losses exceed over $500 billion

1988 Pan Am Flight 103 explodes over Lockerbie, Scotland, killing 259 people— possibly caused by Libyan terrorists

1989 The Cold War ends; the Berlin Wall comes down reuniting East and West Germany

Chinese troops in Beijing's Tiananmen Square, kill hundreds, halting a move toward democracy

Communist leader Nicolae Ceausescu's death reveals Romania's inhumane conditions

Poland's free elections result in "Solidarity's" parliamentary majority, ending communist rule

IMPORTANT ADVANCES IN SCIENCE AND TECHNOLOGY

1981 Acquired Immune Deficiency Syndrome, *AIDS,* a deadly disease with no cure, is discovered

IBM introduces the first widely accepted PC, (personal computer)

1982 Sally Ride becomes the first woman astronaut in space

Time Magazine names the computer "Machine of the Year," instead of a "Man of the Year"

1983 Sony and Philips, market music on compact discs or CD's, a new high quality digital format

Pioneer is the first man-made object to leave the solar system

1985 Expedition goes 13,000 feet under the North Atlantic to find the wreck of *Titanic,* sunk in 1912

1986 Shuttle *Challenger* explodes after liftoff, killing all seven, including civilian teacher Christa McAuliffe.

A nuclear reactor accident at Chernobyl, in the Ukraine, spreads radioactive waste

1987 Chlorofluorocarbon, chlorine, fluorine and carbon, are believed to be damaging the ozone layer

1988 "The Greenhouse Effect," carbon dioxide trapping the sun's rays, may be causing global warming

1989 *World Wide Web,* Internet sites interconnected with text, images and sound is invented

The *Voyager 2* spacecraft, gathers data about the planet Neptune and its moons

The Supreme Court rules flag burning, a form of free speech, protected by the first Amendment

SPOTLIGHT ON THE WORLD OF ENTERTAINMENT

1980 Former Beatle, John Lennon is killed by an obsessed fan outside his apartment in New York City

450 million watch the nighttime soap opera *Dallas* to learn "Who Shot J.R.?" the show's loveable villain

1981 Music Television (MTV) first all-music network airs music videos geared to attract youth

1982 Michael Jackson's record-breaking album *Thriller*, features horror film star Vincent Price

Alice Walker publishes *The Color Purple*, about a black women overcoming adversity

Composer Andrew Lloyd Webber captivates Broadway with *Cats*, based on T.S. Eliot's book

1983 *The Day After*, a movie depicting the horror of nuclear war, airs on television

Millions watch the 251st and last episode of the Korean War based comedy-drama *M*A*S*H*

1984 William Gibson coins the phrase "cyberspace" in his novel *Neuromancer*

1985 Bob Geldof's "Live Aid" concert raises millions for starving people in Africa

1986 Rap music, rhymed verses chanted in forceful repetitive rhythms, becomes popular

1987 Toni Morrison's *Beloved*, a haunting tale of slavery before the Civil War, is published

Les Miserables, based on Victor Hugo's novel opens on Broadway

$53.9 million is paid for Vincent van Gogh's *Irises*

1988 Tom Cruise and Dustin Hoffman star in *Rain Man*, a movie about autism

1989 Rushdie's *Satanic Verses*, a portrait of the prophet Mohammed, provokes threats on his life

The Simpsons, an anti-family cartoon sitcom makes its debuts on television

Self-portrait of Pablo Picasso sells for $47.8 million, the most ever paid for a portrait

SPORTS' HIGHLIGHTS

1980 U.S. hockey team, 20 young players astonishingly win the gold at Lake Placid Winter Olympics

Speed skater, Eric Heiden wins five Gold Medals at the Winter Olympics

Sweden's Bjorn Borg defeats American tennis player, John McEnroe at Wimbledon

1981 Baseball strike lasts 58 days, forces season to be split in two-1st half leaders vs 2nd half winners

1983 Oakland A's Ricky Henderson sets the single season stolen base record with 130

1984 Hockey's New York Islanders win their fourth straight Stanley Cup

1985 Pete Rose's 4,192nd hit passes Ty Cobb's record making him baseball's all-time hit leader

1986 Boston Red Sox, one strike away from their first World Series title since 1918, lose on an error

Jack Nicklaus wins his sixth career Masters, and his 70th PGA Tournament victory

1987 Martina Navratilova achieves a new tennis record, winning her eighth Wimbledon title

1988 Hockey's Edmonton Oilers win their fourth consecutive Stanley Cup

San Francisco earthquake postpones the World Series between the San Francisco Giants and Oakland A's

Pete Rose is banned from baseball for gambling

OTHER INTERESTING FACTS

1980 Mt. St. Helen's, a thought-to-be dormant volcano in Washington state, erupts unexpectedly

RUBICK'S CUBE, a colorful puzzle cube with over 43 quintillion possibilities is the craze

For the first time in history women graduate from military service academies

Designer jeans, denim pants with designer labels, become a fashion statement

1981 The video game craze is propelled by popular animated characters controlled by the players

Sandra Day O'Connor becomes the first woman Supreme Court Justice

Millions of TV viewers watch the storybook wedding of Britain's Prince Charles to Lady Diana

1982 *USA Today,* a national daily newspaper debuts

Cyanide tampered TYLENOL, an over the counter aspirin substitute, kills seven people

EPCOT Center, a futuristic park opens in Orlando, Florida at *Walt Disney World*

1983 CABBAGE PATCH dolls, plain looking dolls with adoption papers become popular

Yuppies are identified as "Young Urban Professionals"

1984 New York becomes the first state to pass a mandatory seat belt law

Exercise, becomes an American obsession, with its slogan, "No Pain, No Gain"

TRIVIAL PURSUIT, a board game of basic knowledge and information is introduced

1985 Crack, a smokeable cocaine, becomes the popular illegal drug

Shoulder pads, used in women's clothing for a broader look, are back in fashion

1986 Over six million people participate in *Hands Across America*, a human chain across the country

1987 Supreme Court rules *Rotary Clubs,* made up of professional and business men, must admit women

Disposable cameras and contact lenses become available

Microsoft's founder Bill Gates becomes the computer world's first billionaire

"Couch Potato" becomes a term referring to one who spends a lot of time in front of the T.V.

1988 Fax Machines, sending documents over telephone lines are the new rage in business

The Ragged look, loose fitting clothing, torn at the knees becomes the fashion statement

Computer viruses developed by hackers, invade systems, destroying information

1989 11 million gallons of oil spills from the Exxon Valdez into Alaska's Prince William Sound

General Colin Powell, is the first black man to become Chairman of the Joint Chiefs of Staff

TEENAGE MUTANT NINJA TURTLES, four human size talking turtles are a big hit with the youth

INTRODUCTION TO THE DECADE

The eighties got off to a good start due to a much improved economy. Technology was moving us along in methods of doing business and in education. But as the decade moved into full gear, happenings abroad created tensions here at home. Our country watched and waited the outcome of events in foreign lands, while we saw new forms of violence erupting in our own neighborhoods. Once again our people pulled together, as we grieved the loss of our gallant space travelers and faced the news of one of our greatest fears. A deadly disease with no cure had reached our shores.

Beth Rubin, shares her feelings in her personal sensitive story, "My Children's Gift Of Courage." Beth says, "AIDS is a disease that respects no one, the young, the old, male, female, and was not always sexually transmitted." In 1983 Beth Rubin was transfused with HIV, infected blood. By 1995, she was in the terminal stages of AIDS, Auto Immune Deficiency Syndrome. Through her faith and the love of her family, her husband, and three daughters, Beth gained both the strength and the courage to continue her valiant fight. In 1999, she lived with her family in Suffern, New York.

My Children's Gift of Courage

Beth Rubin

A forty-five-year-old woman with light brown hair and blue eyes, of Irish descent, a married mother of three young girls and a medical professional living in the suburbs—not your image of someone struggling to live with AIDS?

Well erase that preconceived image. I am that person. The AIDS virus didn't care where I was from, what I looked like or how well I was educated. It had the chance to infect me and it did. Moreover, this non-discriminating organism has taken advantage of that chance hundred of thousands of times the world over, infecting unborn children to the world-renowned. Furthermore, of no concern to the virus is the mode of transmission that accompanies that chance, be it high risk behaviors or blood transfusions.

In the end, the AIDS virus is only interested in two things, its self propagation and survival. It didn't matter to the AIDS virus that Rock Hudson, who succumbed to the disease in 1985, was the movie star heart-throb of women across America in the late 1950's and early 1960's. Of no consequence to the virus was the fact that Liberace, who was perhaps the most outstanding showman of the 1950's through the mid 1980's, produced magical music as his diamond studded fingers danced over the piano keys.

Another notable, Arthur Ashe contracted HIV, the virus that causes AIDS, from a blood transfusion in 1983. This African American was a husband and father, and a Wimbledon tennis champion. But once again the virus didn't care. He died on February 6, 1993 at the age of 49.

I, like Arthur Ashe, was transfused with HIV positive blood in 1983. The blood was ordered during surgery because I have a blood clotting disorder called Von Willebrand's disease. I'm no celebrity, but I am the only mother my three children have and I am not about to give up my battle to survive!

Twelve years have passed since that catastrophic day when I won the AIDS lottery and started losing my life. Now, I am well for only fleeting moments in time. The life threatening diseases are hitting me progressively harder and with decreasing warnings.

Just yesterday, I was at our campsite in upstate New York with my husband and our three young daughters. We enjoyed each others company as we walked along an unspoiled woodland trail. A fuzzy warm cover of deep blue, early autumn sky blanketed us while the filtered rays of the sun, like nature's spotlights, danced off the tangled bushes kneeling at the roots of the mighty trees that reached up to heaven. The sweet fragrances of the last blooms of summer filled our nostrils while the first fallen leaves of the season crunched beneath our feet. Songbirds trilled background music to add to our enjoyment of the day.

Yet, today is nothing like yesterday. I am back in the Pulmonary Isolation Room on the AIDS floor of a New York City hospital. My family has left me for the evening and I am alone with my illness. The only canopy above me is the water stained white ceiling of my sterile prison. The only blanket covering me is the white woven cotton thermal on my bed. The only filtered rays of the sun that I see are those that have passed through my window after having been reflected by the steel and chrome detail on the Chrysler building. The disagreeable smell of disinfectant has replaced the exhilarating fragrance of flowers. The tiled floor is cold and devoid of texture beneath my feet. And, lastly instead of listening to lovely songs, sung by the birds of the forest, my ears are constantly assaulted by the growling sounds of the air purifier above my head.

I know that I have AIDS related pneumonia for the fifth time. I'm burning up with fever, I can't stop coughing and I'm gasping for air. And of course, it has run through my mind that I might never leave this hospital. Because my doctor isn't so sure about the roots of my current disease, he has scheduled a bronchoscopy for tomorrow. It was only three weeks ago when I swore that I would never undergo that barbaric procedure again—with all of its disagreeable components. In particular, I would not allow some specialist to pass a rubber hose into my lungs to diagnose my type of pneumonia. And now, tomorrow, I have to go through it all again.

You might think this is the worst day of my life, when in fact, the most heart rendering day associated with my AIDS experience, was the day I told my three little girls that I was infected with the Human Immunodeficiency Virus.

It was a number of years ago on a frigid February day, that I had visited my AIDS counselor, Mary's office. "What would you like to talk about today?" asked Mary, her granny glasses reflecting the rays of the bright afternoon sun.

"It's what I have to talk about today," I sighed, my heart breaking apart. "Until now, I have shielded my children from my horrific secret, hoping to shield them from the pain as long as possible."

"Go on."

"The pain of not having their mother around to kiss them goodnight, or help them pick out their prom dresses or wedding gowns. I know that my time will soon run out. But how can I bring myself to tell them? When can I bring myself to tell them?"

"You will know when the right time arrives," Mary answered. "It will not be an easy time but it will be the right time."

"I'm afraid their lives will forever be divided into two parts; the time before they knew about Mom's illness and the time after," I sobbed.

"They will be able to go on, just as you have," replied Mary. "They will derive their strength from you."

I was emotionally drained and trembled with anxiety as I started my drive home. Strains of Bobby McFerrin's "Don't Worry Be Happy," assaulted my ears from the speaker of the car radio and I immediately turned it off. How dare he? I thought.

Arriving home, I wiped any signs of tears from my eyes and proceeded to the kitchen. There, my three innocent daughters were sitting around our big farm table enjoying an after school snack. They were so alike yet so different. Tammy, 16 years old, whose long golden brown curls obscured her big blue eyes, was daintily pouring herself a glass of milk. Candace, 12 years old, with her bowl cut reddish auburn hair, looked up at me with a sparkle in her huge hazel eyes. She was dunking her Oreo cookies and gobbling them down as the milk and chocolate crumbs formed a ring around her mouth. Sandy, 10 years old, named for the color of her hair, peeked out from under her fluffy bangs.

"Having a party girls?"

Tammy took a sip of milk then asked suspiciously, "Where were you Mom?" as she stared me straight in the eye.

"Maybe she's having an affair," giggled Candace with the look of the devil in her eye.

Sandy looked coyly over at Candace and they all broke into laughter bubbling milk all over their faces.

It was at that moment, I heard a voice inside say, "This is the right time." My heart began to burn and I eased myself into a chair.

"No girls, I'm not having an affair, but I am going to tell you where I have been going and it's not going to be easy."

"What's the matter, Mommy?" Candace asked as she placed her young hand on mine.

"Girls, do you remember when I had an operation in the city a long time ago?" My head clouded in a surreal nightmare, the words came to me slowly, "I was given some blood, but there had been a problem with it."

"What kind of a problem?" asked Tammy nervously.

Pressure built behind my eyes as I fought back the tears. "It was contaminated."

"With what?" cried Tammy as she jumped to her feet.

"With HIV," I sobbed, choking on my words.

"You mean you got AIDS?" Tammy screamed hysterically.

I looked over at Candace whose tears were mixing with the Oreo cookie crumbs as they rolled past the corners of her mouth. Then, my eyes turned to little Sandy who was crying because everyone else was crying.

"No, I don't have AIDS right now; maybe sometime in the far, far future, but not now. We will take trips to the park, like always and celebrate many more wonderful times together; Christmas and birthdays and super times that you can't even imagine!" Praying that these times would come to pass, I gathered my children around me, kissed them and held them tight and even managed a small smile to further calm their fears. Yet, deep down, I knew that my charade had fooled no one.

I had just ripped open all our hearts and watched all our dreams for the future, like so many beautiful balloons, drift up and away from our empty hearts. Even though we did go to the park, celebrate Christmas and birthdays and have some super times together, the far, far future arrived far too soon.

Today lying here in the hospital, is just one more day in my increasingly uphill battle to survive. I know the AIDS related pneumonia routine by heart. Sometime, before the sunrise tomorrow, I will have a night sweat when my fever plummets to near normal and my body will be covered in an arctic bath that will chill my entire being to the bone. Tomorrow morning, an aide will wrap me up like a container of toxic waste and wheel me on a stretcher to that room where the doctor will lower a rubber hose into my lungs. Next will come the intravenous treatments with side effects as vile and dangerous as any cancer chemotherapy drug.

As usual, I will pray for help to get through each day. Furthermore, I will take advantage of every treatment that is offered to me, whatever the consequences, in hopes of hanging onto the golden thread of life until some miracle drug comes along. After all, whatever happens to me now could never rival the torment of the day that I told my children that I had been infected with HIV.

Remembering their gift of courage, I can cling to the golden thread of life, hoping to walk free again, with my children in the woods under that canopy of deep blue sky while the birds of the forest sing our song.

Conclusion of the Decade

AIDS information and awareness had increased by conclusion of the decade and Americans faced the realization that this was not just a homosexual disease. The end of the decade brought more advances in technology, but Americans were coping with the up and down economy. Domestic violence was still prevalent and foreign concerns were still affecting us. A new word "terrorist" put fear in our hearts. While freedom rang out in distant countries and the world got smaller through use of the Internet, standards of living had improved greatly for most Americans. When we marched into the nineties, the economy was on an upswing and we believed it would bring a better world for all human beings. Little did we suspect that our secure position in the world and the technological advances we had made, would bring new nightmares.

1990's

10

A Time For Looking Back...
A Time For Looking Forward

1990-1999

A world connected in fears and hopes . . .
remembering our past . . .
as the new century dawns.

Memorable Events of the Decade

PRESIDENTS AND THEIR FIRST LADIES

1990–1993 41st George Bush   First Lady Barbara Pierce
1993–1999 42nd William J. Clinton   First Lady Hillary Rodham

MAJOR EVENTS OF THE UNITED STATES AND WORLD HISTORY

1990 Political prisoner Nelson Mandela is freed from captivity in South Africa after 27 years

Saddam Hussein orders his Iraqi army to invade Kuwait, a tiny oil rich nation

President Bush sends U.S. troops to protect Saudi Arabia

1991 President Bush orders Operation Desert Storm, an attempt to halt Saddam Hussein's aggression

Soviet Union ended, Boris Yeltsin becomes the Russian Republics first freely elected President

Clarence Thomas confirmed as Supreme Court Justice despite accusations of sexual harassment

Yugoslavia President Milosevic engages in "ethnic cleansing" to rid his people of all non-Serbs

Supreme Court backs a previous ruling allowing women the right to have an abortion

Berlin once again becomes the capital of a reunified Germany

1992 U.S. helps to bring peace to war torn Bosnia

1993 Apartheid, strict racial segregation and discrimination against non-whites ends in South Africa

Terrorists bomb the World Trade Center in New York City, leaving a hole seven stories deep

Palestinian Liberation Organization leader Arafat and Israeli Prime Minister Rabin agree on peace

1994 Blacks vote for the first time in South African election—Nelson Mandela elected President

1995 The federal building in Oklahoma City is bombed in an act of terrorism, leaving 168 dead

A Time For Looking Back . . . A Time For Looking Forward 139

1997 Princess Diana, of England is killed in a car crash

After 150 years of British rule, Hong Kong is returned to China

1998 President Clinton is accused of having improper relations with a White House intern

1999 Serb massacres of Kosovans to stop separatist activity results in NATO bombing raids

IMPORTANT ADVANCES IN SCIENCE AND TECHNOLOGY

1990 Hubble Telescope orbits 380 miles above the earth for observation, discovery and to return data

HyperText Markup Language, HTML, programming for the Internet is invented

Janet Adkins becomes Dr. Jack Kevorkian's first assisted suicide

Fossil skeleton of *Tyrannosaurus Rex* found in South Dakota

1991 Companies IBM, Apple and Motorola team up to produce the first power computer chip

1992 12 million people worldwide have died of AIDS

1993 First successful cloning; copying genes from one cell to another of human embryos

Development of the first Web Browser, that enables access and display of data on the Web

1994 Jim Clark and Marc Andreessen start Netscape, a web browser provider

1995 DVD, Digital Video Disc becomes the next step in home viewing enhancement

1997 Scientists clone, duplicate, a sheep named *Dolly*

Pathfinder space mission sends photos of Mars back to Earth

1998 Viagra, a prescription medication to cure male impotence is the rage

Former Astronaut, now Senator, John Glenn, returns to space at the age of 77

1999 Last minute scramble to prevent Y2K, year 2000 computer glitch, disaster

The stock market closes the century over 10,000

SPOTLIGHT ON THE WORLD OF ENTERTAINMENT

1990 $100 million art theft at Isabella Stewart Museum in Boston

Ken Burns' documentary *The Civil War* is an 11 hour epic created for public television

$82.5 million is paid for *Portrait of Dr. Gachet* by Vincent van Gogh

Dances with Wolves, a Civil War soldier interacting with the Indians learns about their culture

Journalist Charles Kuralt writes about his experiences in *A Life on the Road*

A Chorus Line, closes on Broadway after 6,137 performances

1991 Nirvana's *Nevermind,* popularizes grunge, creating a fashion statement for sloppiness

The Silence of the Lambs, uses a psychopath, "cannibal" killer to catch another killer

Walter Annenberg leaves his $1 billion art collection to the Metropolitan Museum of Art

J.F.K., the movie, looks at the details of the assassination of President Kennedy in Dallas

Scarlett—The Sequel to Margaret Mitchell's Gone With The Wind is published

1992 Mona van Duyn becomes the first women poet laureate

Rush Limbaugh's *The Way Things Ought To Be* tackles social and political issues

1993 *Men Are From Mars Women Are From Venus,* communicating and getting what you want

Jurassic Park disturbs the natural order as dinosaurs are brought to life for amusement

Schindler's List glorifies a German who defied Hitler and helped hide Jews in Nazi Germany

1994 *Zlata's Diary*—13-year-old, Zlata Filipovic describes her families horrors in war torn Sarajevo

1995 Amazon.com opens its virtual doors, using the Internet to change the book buying experience

1996 Oprah Winfrey recommends book selection—*The Deep End Of The Ocean* on her TV show

Rent premiers off Broadway as its author Jonathan Larsen dies

1997 Angela's Ashes recounts Frank McCourt's childhood memories of New York City and Ireland

1998 Julie Taymor's new techniques bring animals to life as *The Lion King*, comes to Broadway

Audiences glimpse Shakespeare, trying to succeed in his career and as *Shakespeare In Love*

1998 *Titanic*, the story of two people falling in love on a ship that will hit an iceberg and sink

1999 Danielle Steel, Stephen King, and John Grisham had more than five best sellers each, in the nineties

Time calls *Chicken Soup For The Soul Series*, "The publishing phenomenon of the decade"

SPORTS' HIGHLIGHTS

1991 Magic Johnson announces he has Human Immunodeficiency Virus, (HIV) which causes AIDS

1992 Duke's Laettner sinks the winning buzzer-beating basket defeating Kentucky in the NCAA game

The Dream Team, which includes professional basketball players, wins the Olympic gold medal

1993 The Buffalo Bills Frank Reich throws four second-half touchdowns, beating the Houston Oilers

Tennis player, Arthur Ashe, dies of AIDS, from a transfusion of tainted blood

Tennis star Monica Seles is attacked and stabbed by a spectator in Germany

Nolan Ryan, with a record 5,714 strike-outs, retires due to an arm injury

1994 Baseball's World Series is canceled due to a labor strike

Figure skater Nancy Kerrigan is attacked to eliminate her from the skating competition

1995 Baltimore Orioles Cal Ripken Jr. breaks Gehrig's record with 2,131 consecutive baseball games

Former Buffalo Bills football player, O.J. Simpson, is found not guilty of murdering his wife and her friend

1997 Bizarre boxing moment, Mike Tyson bites off a piece of Evander Holyyfield's ear in title bout

Multi-ethnic golfer, Tiger Woods, sets a new course record winning the Masters Tournament

1998 Mark McGuire, breaks the single season home-run record by hitting #70

Chicago Bulls, Michael Jordan, sinks the game-winning goal, his sixth NBA title, in his last game

1999 Brandi Chastain leads the U.S. Soccer team to the Women's World Cup

Golfer, Payne Stewart, dies in a plane crash, four months after winning the U.S. Open

Denver Broncos win their second consecutive Super Bowl and Quarterback John Elway retires

New York Yankee, David Cone, pitches a perfect game on Yogi Berra Day at Yankee Stadium

The New York Yankees win their 25th World Series

OTHER INTERESTING FACTS

1990 Population - 270 million people in America

94% of Americans own telephones

98% of Americans own televisions

Broccoli is banned from the White House menu by President Bush

McDonald's, the fast food hamburger chain opens in Moscow

1991 It is estimated that over 300,000 Americans are homeless

1992 U.S. unemployment hits an eight year high

1993 The Holocaust Memorial Museum opens in Washington D.C. to honor victims of Nazi Germany

It is estimated that over 12 million Americans use cellular phones

Over 100,000 gays, (homosexuals), march in Washington for equal rights to end discrimination

Florida attorney, Janet Reno, becomes the first woman U.S. Attorney General

Bombing at the World Trade Center kills five people

1994 AIDS, Acquired Immune Deficiency Syndrome epidemic reportedly infects over 15 million

A Time For Looking Back . . . A Time For Looking Forward 143

Questions arise about the President and Mrs. Clinton's involvement in an Arkansas land deal

The Original nine BEANIE BABIES, hand sized bean bag type stuffed animals, are the craze

1996 Gary Kasparov, chess master defeats IBM's Deep Blue computer, 4 games to 2

1999 Time magazine names Albert Einstein "Person of the Century"

World population hits 6 billion

13% of the U.S. population is over 65—as compared with 4% in 1900

Booming stock market propels economic indicators to 40 year high

INTRODUCTION TO THE DECADE

As we soared into the nineties on wings of new technology, we were still discovering our past and learning how the decisions we had made were affecting our lives. The environment was causing havoc and concern, while diseases that had been long forgotten were reappearing. Another concern, was that as we moved forward in areas of cloning and computers, would we loose the human component? The world peace we enjoyed in the eighties, had left us with a feeling of security but as the world got smaller, we learned how a country, far, far away could make us all fear for our lives.

As America was drawn into the conflicts a world away, we bonded together. We watched as our troops were bombarded nightly and kept them in our thoughts hoping they would return safely to a free world. "Remembering Desert Storm" is our salute to the many brave men and women who left their homes and families to fight for freedom and stand up for the way of life we hold so dear.

Remembering Desert Storm

*Francine R. Cefola
and Bobbi R. Madry*

WE NEVER THOUGHT OUR SOLDIERS
WOULD AGAIN GO OFF TO WAR
BUT THE 90'S SAW THEM MARCHING,
WHAT WAS THIS AGGRESSION FOR
OUR MEN AND WOMEN SERVING
DYING IN A FOREIGN LAND
THE PERSIAN GULF ... SADDAM HUSSEIN ...
WE FACED WAR ONCE AGAIN

THEY BRAVELY FOUGHT THE BATTLES
DEFENDING ALL OUR HUMAN RIGHTS
THEY ESCAPED THE ENEMY'S FIRE
THE BOMBS FALLING THROUGH THE NIGHTS
WE GRIEVE FOR THOSE WHOSE TURN IT WAS
TO SUFFER ... AND TO DIE
WE'LL SHED OUR TEARS AND PRAY FOR THEM
AS WE BID THEM SAD GOODBYE

AND NOW AS WE REMEMBER
THE SOLDIERS OF DESERT STORM
THEY GAVE THEIR LIVES THAT WE MIGHT LIVE
AND KEPT THE WORLD FROM HARM

REMEMBER NOW, EACH ONE OF THEM,
SAY THEY DID IT JUST FOR ME
THEY FOUGHT THE FIGHT FOR GOOD AND RIGHT,
SO OTHERS MIGHT BE FREE

Introduction to the Story

Whether we need a release from what is going on in the world, or just want to relax, baseball is truly an American institution. Millions of fans passionately root for their favorite teams from April to October each year. One such fan, Carianne Carleo-Evangelist, has shared her love of baseball and her all-American enthusiasm for her team, The New York Yankees. In 1999, she was at Nazareth College in Rochester, studying Economics and International Studies, Carianne has been a Yankees fan since she attended her first baseball game in the mid eighties at Yankee Stadium. Her favorite player was Don Mattingly. Carianne's story, "Chasing the Dream . . . The Life of a Yankee Fan," celebrates not only the Yankees of today, but also pays tribute to the entire Yankees Dynasty, the "Team of the Century," which won 35 Pennants and 25 World Championships Series.

Chasing the Dream . . . The Life of a Yankee Fan

Carianne Carleo-Evangelist

People always speak of the Yankee dynasties of years past. It was 1920 when Babe Ruth was sold by the Boston Red Sox to the New York Yankees for $100,000.00, and the "Curse of the Bambino," began. From that time, the Red Sox did not play in a World Series until 1946, and then they lost.

With the addition of the "Babe," the Yankees began moving toward their incredible future. Under manager Miller Huggins, Babe Ruth and the Yankees flourished. In 1925 Lou Gehrig took his position at first base and the Ruth/Gehrig legend began. Catcher, Bill Dickey joined the Yankees in 1928. During Huggins' years, 1918-1929, the Yankees established themselves in the baseball world winning three World Series Championships, 1923, 1927 and 1928.

Joe McCarthy took over as field manager of the Yankees in 1931. In 1936, Joe DiMaggio donned his pinstripes and headed for left field but, by 1937 he had taken up his position, patrolling center field. The remaining McCarthy years saw the addition of shortstop, Phil Rizzuto and seven more World Championships: 1932, 1936, 1937, 1938, 1939, 1941 and 1943. The Yankees became the first team to win four championships in a row.

The years 1949–1960, when the Yankees were successfully managed by Casey Stengel, added more talent patrolling the field of "The House that Ruth Built," as Yankee Stadium came to be called. In the outfield Mickey Mantle took over for DiMaggio and Hank Bauer alternated in right field until 1960 when Roger Maris took that position. Whitey Ford was on the pitching mound, Yogi Berra and Elston Howard were catching. Names like Bill Skowron, first base, Billy Martin and Bobby Richardson, second, Tony Kubek, shortstop, Clete Boyer, third, Gil McDougald, second and third base, helped the Yankees to win seven more World Series Championships, and become the first team to win five championships in a row.

The Yankees won again in 1961 and 1962, under manager Ralph Houk, and then a horrible drought occurred until they won the 1977 World Series, under manager Billy Martin, against the Los Angeles Dodgers; once again the Yankees were making history. Their relief pitcher, Sparky Lyle who is designated to relieve the starting pitcher during a game, became the first American League reliever to win the prestigious Cy Young Award. Then in 1978, with players like, pitcher Ron Guidry, Chris Chamblis at first base, Willie Randolph at second, Graig Nettles, third base, Bucky Dent, shortstop, Reggie Jackson in the outfield, and Bob Lemon now managing the team, once again, the Yankees met Los Angeles Dodgers in the World Series and swept them in four games.

A Time For Looking Back . . . A Time For Looking Forward

Through the 80's the Yankees' success was fleeting and tragedy claimed the life of former player and manager, Billy Martin, who died in a car accident, December 1989. But when Buck Showalter became manager in the 1990's, hopes were high, until a players' strike dampened the fans' spirits and put a halt to the 1994 season. The strike was settled and the 1995 season began with a degree of success. This was the first year of the Wild Card; brought about to give more teams a chance at a spot in the playoffs. The Yankees' spirits were high until August when 1950's and 1960's center fielder, number 7, Mickey Mantle, died. In their grief, many Yankees and their fans were reminded of another August when tragedy hung over the stadium. Thurman Munson, Yankee catcher in the late 70's, who in the 1976 World Series, hit .529 in four games against the Reds, had died in a plane crash in August 1979.

But in true Yankees' fashion, tribute was paid to Mantle and the team played ball. The Yankees won the Wild Card spot and played the winner of the American League West, the Seattle Mariners, in the first round of the playoffs, a best of five games, called the Division Series. But the Yankees lost all the games in Seattle and this series. The fans, though very disappointed, knew their team had done well and looked toward next year.

The off-season brought the retirement of the "The Hit Man," #23, Yankee first baseman, Donald Arthur Mattingly. Next, Buck Showalter announced plans to join the staff of the Arizona Diamondbacks. Then infielder Randy Velarde and catcher Mike Stanley were leaving. Fans worried how the 1996 season would play out with so many core members gone.

But things began to change. Trades were made and the Yankees got relief pitcher Graeme Lloyd, while first baseman Tino Martinez replaced Mattingly. The Yankees hired Joe Torre as the manager and filled the catcher's spot with Joe Girardi. The new shortstop would be a young kid from Kalamazoo, Michigan, named Derek Jeter.

The 1996 season started with a degree of success. May 14 was a day to remember; the Yankees were playing Seattle at Yankee Stadium and facing a former Yankee, Sterling Hitchcock, who had been traded for Martinez and Lloyd. I was in Yankee Stadium that day to see Yankee Pitcher, Doc Gooden, who came up with the New York Mets, and had been plagued by drug problems, pitch a no hitter. To the delight of the fans, he never allowed a batter to get a base hit.

The Yankees stayed in first place for most of the '96 season, despite a late season slide. They clinched the East title and their playoff run began. Winning their final playoff game against the Baltimore Orioles sent the Yankees to the World Series against Atlanta. The Series did not get off to a good start with the Yankees losing the first two games at home. However, things looked up when the team swept the three games against the Braves in Atlanta and returned home for Game 6. The Yankees and their fans hoped Game 6 would decide the series.

The game was scheduled for Saturday night and it seemed as if all America was tuned in. Tensions were high for Yankee fans. It was the top of the 9th, the Braves were down to their last out. The pitch, swing, popped up to third, but it goes into the seats; still two outs and Yankee fans continue to hold their breath. Another pitch, another pop up to third, but this time it stays in play. Yankee third baseman Charlie Hayes, makes the play and the Yankees are again World Champs. What a celebration! New York hadn't seen a sports championship since the New York Giants, football team, won the Superbowl in the early 90's and hadn't seen a baseball championship since the New York Mets won in '86. New York paraded the team through the "Canyon of Heroes," the traditional route ticker tape parades take through Manhattan.

In 1997 the Yankees did make it to the playoffs, however, they suffered a crushing loss in the Division Series to Cleveland. But in the true spirit of being a Yankee fan, we looked forward to 1998 with the belief that it would be even better.

The 1998 season started with losing being the name of their game, then at their first home game, the Yankees scored 17 runs resetting the tone for what would be a Miracle Year. Many of the players were having the best year of their playing career and the team was running away with their division. 1998 also saw a feat rarely achieved in baseball, even in the storied history of the New York Yankees. Pitcher David Wells, tossed a perfect game, not allowing a player from the opposing team to get on base, either by a base hit, a walk, or an error. A perfect game in a perfect season. The team's hot streak lasted through the remainder of the season and into the playoffs landing them in the World Series opposite the San Diego Padres. The Yankees swept San Diego in four straight games. More celebrations erupted in New York for these World Series Champs, who had had a phenomenal season. The fans looked onward to 1999, but few believed the Yankees could ever recapture their success. Their team had won more games than any team had ever won, in any previous baseball season. These Yankees were being compared with the greatest teams of the past, the 1927 Yankees and the 1961 Yankees. Which Yankee team was the best of all time? The arguments ensued; there of course is no right answer.

The off season between 1998 and 1999 brought the most exciting as well as unexpected news. A trade was made with Toronto. The Yankees, surprisingly, sent pitcher David Wells, of "perfect game" fame, to the Toronto Blue Jays and received pitcher Roger Clemens, a five time Cy Young Award Winner and a former Red Sox pitcher. This shocked the fans and the baseball world. Was it the "Curse of the Bambino" revisited?

Before the season began, fans had some good and some bad news. Yogi Berra and owner, George Steinbrenner, settled their long time feud. Yogi would be returning to the stadium for the first time since he was fired as manager in the 1980's. Sadly though, we learned Manager Joe Torre and designated hitter, Darryl Strawberry both had cancer. Then in early March, we learned of the death of Joe DiMaggio, the Yankee Clipper; voted the best player of the first half of the 20th. Century. The memory of this outstanding outfielder who could do everything and make it look easy, had long been a symbol of the Yankees, even after he stopped playing. In his honor, the Yankees wore his number 5, on their uniforms all through the season.

The Yankees were not as dominant in 1999, but on one weekend in July, when the major news was the crash of John Fitzgerald Kennedy Jr.'s plane, the Yankees made history again. July 18th, Yogi Berra Day at Yankee Stadium, pitcher David Cone was on the mound against the Montreal Expos. He was pitching a perfect game; then a long rain delay—he returned to the mound, faced and retired twenty-seven Expos batters; a second perfect game in a little over a year. In modern baseball history, there had been fewer than twenty perfect games and here the Yankees had two in two seasons. What a day for the Yankees, their fans and Yogi.

The season progressed and the Yankees won the division title and started their playoffs. Triumphant, they awaited the results of the Atlanta-Mets Series. New Yorkers began to wonder whether the World Series would be a "Subway Series, " which got its name because both teams and their fans could hop on the subway to get to either stadium. New Yorkers reminisced about five 1950's World Series between the Yankees and the then New York Giants, or the then Brooklyn Dodgers. However, Atlanta prevailed and we were left with a rematch of 1996.

The Series began strong. The Yankees took the first two games, and fans began to whisper about 1996. Their whispers turned to shouts when the Yankees emerged victorious in 1999 once again. New York brought out the brooms again as the Yankees swept Atlanta in four games. What a celebration!

The Yankees—a truly remarkable team, whose history dates back to 1903, won their first pennant in 1923. Within the next 76 years, they had won 35 pennants and 25 world championships. They won almost half of the pennants available in that period of time and almost one third of the World Championships. No other team can claim such success. Who knows what the Yankees are capable of achieving in the next year, the next decade, the next century or the next millennium? As for me, "This is one fan who is anxiously waiting."

INTRODUCTION TO THE STORY

When future generations look back on the events of the 20th. Century, they may smile, at the fears and apprehensions their ancestors felt, as technology advanced at such a dizzying pace. From the invention of the automobile and airplane to landing a man on the moon, we were riding on a wave of computerized advances that tied the world together as never before. In fact, there were more advances during the past 100 years than in all preceding centuries. Yet, as we approached the new millennium, we were asking some serious questions. Would our computerized world come crashing down in disaster as the clock struck 12 on the eve of the year 2000?

Many people had seen the letters Y2K, meaning year 2000, in news articles, magazines and on the nightly news . . . and many paid no attention. Their thinking was, after all it's just another year. Others became so concerned, they began preparing for a major global disaster by stocking up on survival gear and supplies, just in case we had to revert to the primitive state of the cave-dwellers. While millions celebrated the coming of the new millennium, throwing caution to the wind, millions more held their breath.

Anthony M. Cefola's story, "The Y2K Nightmare," relates how serious this issue was in 1999. A graduate of Ithaca College, Anthony has a Bachelor of Science Degree in Sports, Information and Communication, with minors in Coaching and Legal Studies. He was involved in the technical side of web pages and web based software as a computer programmer-specialist who also designed web-sites. Anthony was also the computer consultant to The Write Source and Golden Quill Press and in 1999, he redesigned the company's web presence upgrading the system including internet publishing.

The Y2K Nightmare

Anthony M. Cefola

From the first time I was introduced to computers as a young child, I was fascinated by them. It intrigued me to learn that computer chips have date timers on them and how the computer relies so heavily on these chips. Major parts of the computer such as: the operating system, power supply, error checking programs, files that make up the computer and anything that has to do with dates—all need to know, to the second, what date it is and what it will be the next second. I later learned that most of these computer chips are 6 digits long, (hard coded so that there are only 6 actual spots on the circuit board inside the system), two for each month, two for the day, and two for the year. This was originally done to save computer space and therefore money, when creating computers. It seemed logical then for companies to do away with anything that didn't seem necessary, therefore, the two digits representing the 19, in 1900 was deemed a waste of time, space and money. The systems creators of the 50's, 60's and 70's didn't worry about the possible repercussions for the future.

As we neared the end of this century, people who understood the mistakes that were made, began to wonder what would happen on 12/31/99 when the computer tried to add one year to the current year and change the date to January 1, 2000. One of two things could happen. First, the computer would try to add 1 to the year '99, which equals 100, but since there are only two spots available and 100 needs 3, the computer would crash and could never work again. Second, the computer would try to add 1 to the year '99 and gets past the 3 digit problem, but when it advances to '00 it thinks it is the year 1900. In this case, most computers would encounter only minor glitches with the system itself, but computer records that are date specific, such as the IRS and FBI, credit cards, banks and other business information, would have a problem because according to the computer, most of the entries would not happen for another 80 to 95 years. Therefore, these very important entries that affect all our lives will either be removed by the computer's error checking system, or will be inaccessible by any program because it believes they haven't happened yet.

So here I sit, concerned about Y2K and what could happen, staring blurry eyed at the computer screen after weeks of preparation, with little rest and running through systems checks to be sure my business and personal computers are prepared. It's 10:30 on New Years' Eve. "I'll just close my eyes, for a moment. . . ." Startled, by some flash of light, I open my eyes. "Wait! What's going on! My computer just shut down." The lights are beginning to flicker—"Oh no!" I look at my watch, it's 12:01. Suddenly the house is completely dark. I pick up the flashlight I had put nearby, just in case. Moving through the house I get to the window only to find the streets and all the houses around are also totally dark. Gathering the candles I had bought and finding matches, I light my way back inside to where the portable radio is. Turning off the flashlight to conserve the batteries, I slump into my chair and wonder. "Is this Y2K? Has it really come?"

Trying not to panic, I began to think—what could be happening. "If Y2K has happened then all government records, including the CIA, FBI and IRS, could be LOST! Everything from criminal records and trial decisions, to possible anti-government activity, that was all on computers could be gone, threatening the security of this and other countries. And what else?

"If it's true, then one of the most serious questions will be the state of nuclear weapons throughout the world. Computer failures could cause anything from launch, or worse, detonation, to deactivation, crippling the warfare power of any nation. Satellite communications failing is another major concern. In today's modernized world, pagers, cell phones, cable TV, global intelligence, NASA, and many others depend on a satellite network in orbit around the earth. Without these, we could be back to smoke signals and Morse code." The thought hits me, "I don't even know Morse code . . . I'd be lost in that world. If the computer systems or power systems have failed, we will be faced with the possibility that information world wide would be lost almost entirely. Without computers to run The Internet, the world's largest research and communication tool would be nonexistent."

Knowing I have to pull myself together and stop speculating, I turn on the radio. There is so much static, I keep turning the dial, back and forth . . . "Oh good," I finally find a station I am able to hear and can pickup parts of a news report. So far from what they say, all airplanes have been grounded or those that were in the air were able to land safely. I breathe a sigh of relief. "Thank Goodness, the airline companies did everything to further their Y2K compliance; hired trained people to fix the problems, paid for the computer patches to deflect as much of the Y2K problem as possible, or in the worst case, kept the planes on the ground."

The announcement I heard next declared a state of emergency. The radio and special services were operating off generators in order to keep the public informed. The government had issued an advisory statement that everyone should remain inside their homes. The announcement went on to say that a curfew had been instituted, "No one, except emergency services personnel would be allowed on the roads."

Locally they advised, that in many areas backup generators had not kicked in and the computers that support the power systems were all down. There was no telling when power would be restored. The announcer concluded by saying, "Our emergency services are being overtaxed and the fire departments, police and hospitals can't keep up with the needs. Let's all pray this nightmare will end soon."

I was feeling scared, apprehensive, fearful and I had some understanding about what could happen. I imagined people who hadn't prepared at all and those who would be taking this lightly. What will happen to them if this doesn't end soon. Panic will surely set in. When the water systems, also controlled by computers, (except with old wells), affecting our drinking and bathing water begin to create serious sanitation and health problems. "How long could we survive without clean water? I guess people will be able to get water from streams or when it rains or snows, but it won't be filtered or processed and that may lead to more health hazards."

By now my teeth are chattering, but I'm not sure if it is from cold or fear. "I'm getting cold just sitting here with these blankets wrapped around me. It's just the middle of winter, this cold weather could last at least until March." I begin to imagine being without heat for all that time. "And the lights. Yes, I have my flashlight and candles, but for how long? We've become so dependent on our comforts, our appliances and machines and now they have all stopped working. The computers have shut down the phone systems, so people have lost touch with family and friends. Without being able to make contact with loved ones and with the loss of our information systems, TV, computers, the internet, it will be even more devastating—there will be widespread panic."

Then I realized, all these problems would also affect the manufacture, marketing and transportation of food and other daily necessities. If deliveries can't be made soon, a lack of food, medicines and health care products will exist. Stores had been running out of non-perishable food for a while, in anticipation of this day, but now, the lack of refrigeration only adds to the growing problem.

"Some people will be able to survive better than others. Those fanatics we all laughed at. They knew how bad this would be. They went ahead and stock-piled non-perishable food, fire wood, batteries, cooking oil lanterns and even guns . . . every possible need to get them through. Most like me, only took minor precautions, having some extra canned and boxed foods, bottled water, candles, flashlight, portable radio and extra batteries. I even made sure to fill my prescriptions, pick up extra dog food, stop at the bank and get cash to last for at least a month. It wasn't until I actually thought about eating the canned food, that I remembered I would need a non-electric can opener. Maybe it was silly to get cash, but I figured banking records could be removed by system errors, causing the financial world much confusion and enabling accounts to be broken into by hackers. Now I realize this cash won't do me much good if there is nothing to buy. Oh how we've become dependent on our computers.

"I didn't think about this but, without computers what would happen to our jobs? Business and industry depended on computer records and would operate totally in the dark and have to shut down. Even the Stock Markets would crash and anyone who had invested money in stocks, bonds and mutual funds could be wiped out." Thoughts of total anarchy ran through my mind. I envisioned governments on every level breaking down, the strong ruling the weak, gangs of people joining together with common fears and thoughts of survival overthrowing what little civilization we might still have. Hoards of starving people would have no fear of a policeman armed with a six-shooter and a flashlight.

These thoughts were really frightening as I sat by candlelight feeling so disconnected from the world, knowing all this was because of computer chips. To think if only they had been able to do something to stop it. My eyes begin to close. All I wanted to do was shut out this nightmare.

I didn't know how long I had been dozing, but when I opened my eyes, I was staring into my computer screen. I looked around. The lights were on and everything seemed to be working. Was I dreaming? I glanced down to the bottom of the computer screen, 11:58. I checked the date, 12/31/99! I turned on my television. Reports of New Years Eve around the world told of no major problems anywhere. There, in my living room, I was watching people crammed into Times Square happily waiting for the arrival of the new year. As the countdown began I watched the ball drop—was it about to begin? There was no stopping it now . . . 5 . . . 4 . . . 3 . . . 2 . . . 1. . . . I closed my eyes in anticipation of the mighty 2000. When I opened them . . . the lights were still on. . . . Did I dream what happened, or is this the dream?

We are happy that our computer geniuses were able to prevent a Y2K disaster, but it could have happened—it could still happen. We shouldn't pretend that Y2K was a hoax. Many small problems did occur. Some companies did lose records. Others took the precautions and changed their infrastructure to prevent problems, but in some cases this only led to other problems.

Have we become too dependent on our machines? We must be aware! We must keep watch!

Conclusion of the Decade

As the clock ticked down the decade and the century, we joined together as one world, holding our breath, and watching to be sure each country entered the new century safely. The world for the first time stood united to celebrate our accomplishments and our hopes for the future. We had begun the decade in fear and watched as technology helped us turn our sights from war to peace and global communication. In space as on the earth, we were moving forward at a rapid pace, even to the world's first landing on Mars. But our advances also had a dark side, as nature rebelled and the strides we had made in technology turned and threatened our environment. We also faced a new, smaller world as the web opened up distant lands, making them as near as a phone call and dot com's were replacing old addresses and ways of doing business. Where would these new advances lead us? Would we learn from past mistakes, benefit from our accomplishments and unite as one world . . . young and old to log on to the tale of this new century . . . bringing us into the future.

We dedicate this Chapter to all the men and women who served our country during the Persian Gulf War to protect our shores and safeguard our country's freedom.

2000's

11

The Twenty First Century and Beyond . . . What Will The Future Bring?

2000

Introduction to the New Century

Perhaps music, more than any other form of communication, has sent messages from one generation to another, and from one decade to another. Blending our cultures, music evokes our emotions; can make us laugh, make us cry and bring cherished memories to mind. Music is a universal language that unites people in a common bond.

Music Through The Century is our contribution to the memories that helped to delight generations of Americans. When we were writing this poem we were experiencing and reliving those times and the music painted a picture of what each decade was like. For your enjoyment, we have put the song titles in bold . . . let the music take you to those days gone by, visualize the times . . . see how many song titles you remember . . . and enjoy the memories they evoke.

Music Through The Century

Bobbi R. Madry and Francine R. Cefola

It's the early 1900's
Music's blooming all around
From Puccini's **Madame Butterfly**
to the new hot Ragtime sound

Immigrants flood to America
Bringing their proud songs to sing
Blending cultures and their music
All singing let freedom ring

Come **Let's Take An Old Fashioned Walk**
Phonograph records are brand new
We'll waltz to **The Merry Widow**
and dance the Tango too

The Twenty First Century and Beyond . . .

A new decade—it's 1910
With Alexander's Ragtime Band
We sang about M-O-T-H-E-R and Danny Boy
K-K-K-Katy got a hand

The news of the Titanic sinking
Income Taxing every dime
War is raging Over There
Prohibition, organized crime

To Keep The Home Fires Burning
Rock-A-Bye Baby to Swannee
But until the war is over
I Ain't Got Nobody, but me

Now comes the Roaring 20's
Making Whoopee made our day
Flappers danced the Charleston
Always, Chasin' the Blues Away

Evolution has its day in court
Women finally get the vote
Still no alcohol to drink
No Stock Market left to quote

Just Button Up Your Overcoat
When Blue Skies turn to gray
Let A Smile Be Your Umbrella
For Jazz is here to stay

And now begins the 30's
Brother Can You Spare A Dime
I feel I'll Never Smile Again
It's Stormy Weather all the time

Depression takes its toll on all
Roosevelt's New Deal brings some hope
The repeal of good old alcohol
Drinking becomes a way to cope

ANYTHING GOES *in the movies*
OVER THE RAINBOW *we can fly*
GET HAPPY *with the* EASTER PARADE
Singing' BLACKBIRD, BYE, BYE

GOD BLESS AMERICA, *it's the 40's*
Big bands play tunes all through the night
So PAPA WON'T YOU DANCE WITH ME
Before you go off to fight

War arrives on Americas Shores
Courtesy of the Japanese
Together we stood—American Style
Together we fought for peace

PRAISE THE LORD AND PASS THE AMMUNITION
Dreaming of a WHITE CHRISTMAS *with you*
So put on a STRING OF PEARLS *my dear*
For I'LL BE SEEING YOU *too*

The 50's rock in with HIGH HOPES
We'll buy some BAUBLES, BANGLES AND BEADS
HOW MUCH IS THAT DOGGIE IN THE WINDOW?
And WHATEVER LOLA WANTS ... OR NEEDS

Korea ends there's peace again
Prosperity as families grow
Civil Rights are seen in black and white
On the nightly television show

Now EVERYTHING'S COMING UP ROSES
SIXTEEN TONS *is a lot of coal*
So Don't Step on my BLUE SUEDE SHOES
As we Lindy to Rock 'n' Roll

We twisted into the 60's
LOVE MAKES THE WORLD GO ROUND
It was DAYS OF WINE AND ROSES
and the Beatles brand new sound

*Kennedy, King and Kennedy
Assassinations, Vietnam War
Students killed while protesting
Then our country cried, No More!*

It was peace, love A HARD DAY'S NIGHT
and a STONED SOUL PICNIC *blast*
I BELIEVE, RESPECT *made a comeback
with a man on the moon at last*

*The 70's brought some good, some bad
That made up the* AMERICAN PIE
We were wishing for THE WAY WE WERE
and disco'd as time flew by

*Watergate's in the spotlight now
What did the President know?
Vietnam ends; celebrating with friends
The '76 Bicentennial Show*

TIME IN A BOTTLE, *just* LET IT BE
I know that I WILL SURVIVE
The CAT'S IN THE CRADLE *there's*
JOY TO THE WORLD, *and I'm* STAYIN' ALIVE

The 80's—we're STARTING OVER
With a CELEBRATION—9 TO 5
WE ARE THE WORLD, *we boasted
It was great to be alive*

*Hostages home, they're free at last
The Berlin Wall comes tumblin' down
Reaganomics and Black Monday
Then AIDS arrived in town*

It's EBONY AND IVORY
Like the WIND BENEATH MY WINGS
We'll SHOUT, *hey,* WE DON'T KNOW MUCH,
or what the future brings

From A Distance in the 90's
You're my Hero in Desert Storm
There must have been Tears In Heaven
As you kept us safe and warm

It's the Internet and World Wide Web
We were threatened with Y2K
The Yankees, our Team of The Century
Baby Boomers led the way

Life was not a Kiss From A Rose
nor a Candle In The Wind
We bet it all on The Power of Love
as the century came to an end

Now as we "TELL IT TO THE FUTURE"
Cherishing old memories
Let's share our songs and stories
Music Through The Centuries

Moving Into the Next Century

As the clocks ticked away the twentieth century, we united to celebrate the old and welcome the new. We stopped to contemplate where we had been and where we were going. We had experienced greatness as a people and as a nation and we had accepted that we still had much to learn about the powers that control our world, nature and the threats that we create. As we look back upon this great Century, we have come from "Wheels and Hooves" to "A Time For Looking Back . . . A Time For Looking Forward," and are moving into the next century with new promises and hopes.

The authors and writers of *TELL IT TO THE FUTURE—Have I Got A Story For You . . . about the Twentieth Century,* have also added their hopes and wishes for the future sharing with you the reader, their wisdom and insight for your enjoyment.

Hopes and Wishes for the Future

1900's

"Care about yourself and set worthwhile goals. Treasure your family and friends because they are more precious than anything else. Always let them know you love and appreciate them."

MARY BIANCHINI

1910's

"God created man and set the world in motion, man has not stopped. The future is anyone's guess, but God alone has the answers."

GEORGIA STRUNK

1920's

"I would like the leaders of the world to promote fair-trading policies and for people to promote a world where peace and prosperity will reign supreme."

LOU BAUM

1930's

BOBBI R. MADRY (SEE FROM THE AUTHORS)

1940's

"My hope is for people to take time and listen with open hearts, and years later, be proud to look to the past."

EILEEN M. FOTI

"My wish for the future is for a world at peace and the eradication of hunger and disease."

JEAN M. OLWELL

1950's

"Today is the future of yesteryear - Honor, respect and enjoy life—as the precious gift it is. Do Your Best and Always Smile."

FRAN TOEPFER

FRANCINE R. CEFOLA (SEE FROM THE AUTHORS)

"Buy a bag of fortune cookies and each day add one saying into your life. Listen with your heart, before you speak your mind And see Love!"

MARILYN BENKLER

"Take care of the earth. Learn how to receive. Love one person, more than you love yourself. Read books about native Americans. Create Art!"

ELLEN ZIEGLER

1960's

"What I want for the future is that we be in harmony with ourselves, so we can enjoy the natural beauty that surrounds us."

ANNE M. OGLE

"Stand by your beliefs—carefully consider issues—Don't let rights and freedoms be legislated away. Let no lives be squandered in halfhearted and unworthy causes."

ROBERT REEG

"It is my prayer that the entire world will embrace the philosophy of Dr. Martin Luther King Jr., and his teachings, making them a reality in the new century."

NAOMI G. ANTHONY

1970's

"May whatever, "Golden Road" you travel, lead you to a special magical place that you will forever cherish in your heart."

THERESA ZARRELLA

1980's

"That HIV will go the way of other dreaded diseases. That people not be judged by what befalls them and appreciate their true blessings."

BETH RUBIN

1990's

"You may find that things change very quickly, just let them go as they may . . . and enjoy what happens."

CARIANNE CARLEO-EVANGELIST

"Find the one you are meant for and never let them go. 'In The End, There Can Be Only One.'"

ANTHONY M. CEFOLA

At a networking meeting of The Write Source Writers' Association the following attendees contributed their wishes to *TELL IT TO THE FUTURE*.

Marilyn Benkler	Jerry Pooler
Lia Binetti	Robert Reeg
Anne Flax	Jack Shapiro
Eileen Foti	Fran Toepfer
Barbara Green	Barbara Werzansky
Claudia Kempton	Stephanie Wolfe
Barbara Plasker	

"Life is beautiful if you take the time to smell the roses; appreciate the present without letting a moment go by unnoticed."

"Don't let unimportant details get in the way of your fulfilling your first love. Be open to all the love that comes into your life—Opportunities are like stepping stones that can lead to a deeper place—Don't be afraid to let your deepest feelings emerge."

From the Authors:

May nations heed
Lessons from the past
And unite the world
In peace at last

May mutual respect
Ever be our guide
To a future we share
With loving pride

                BOBBI R. MADRY

If the world stopped tomorrow
   would you say
I was happy for having lived today?
Then stop for a moment and think,
   before you go on
the direction you've decided upon,
As the world spins again,
   I hope you won't wait
Decide, then Do It Now!
   Before it is too late!

              FRANCINE R. CEFOLA

We invite you to add your words of wisdom and insight
as you write your wishes for the future . . . .

The Twenty First Century and Beyond . . .

WHAT WILL OUR LEGACY BE?

Can we go beyond this point building on the great knowledge we have gained, while always being mindful of our past accomplishments as well as our mistakes? Can we create a world for future generations that at the end of the twenty first century will be looked upon as a gift from the past, as we in *TELL IT TO THE FUTURE* acknowledge the gifts of those who have gone before us.

We hope you have enjoyed reading *TELL IT TO THE FUTURE—Have I Got A Story For You . . . about the Twentieth Century*. We hope you have gained even more appreciation for our country and all its citizens and how we have developed into the world we see today. We look forward to your comments about your favorite stories and decade.

Share Your Thoughts
Golden Quill Press invites you to share your thoughts, impressions and hopes. Your favorite memories of the 20th. century and best decade and why. We will share those responses on our web site- www.goldenquillpress.com at a new page called TELL IT TO THE FUTURE So, add your thoughts Today!
email: info@goldenquillpress.com

Have you ever wanted to write a book? Visit our web site and see all the programs available to help you see your dream come true! www.goldenquillpress.com/writingservices.html

And Don't forget to **check out other books by Golden Quill Press** at: www.goldenquillpress.com/bookstore.html

AUTHORS' BIOGRAPHIES

BOBBI R. MADRY is Educational Director of The WriteSource and Golden Quill Press. She has served as author and senior editor of educational publications and director of human relations programs for major New York City publishers. She writes book reviews for national magazines and has authored several books, including, **"Love Makes the Difference," "NewHorizons,"and "How To Write your Book."** She has also served as Associate Publisher for a Rockland newspaper where she was a mentor to aspiring writers and has received numerous awards for writing and community service. As a writing consultant/editor Bobbi assists others in writing and publishing their works. She also teaches creative writing and poetry. She holds degrees in the arts and behavioral sciences.

FRANCINE R. CEFOLA is a writer, editor and publisher for The Write Source and Golden Quill Press. She has developed writing programs for all ages, including seniors and teens. Francine has been an author for over forty years and has received many writing awards for poetry and short stories. She has co-authored,**"NewHorizons," and "How to Write Your Book," and has edited and helped publish numerous books**. Working with children for many of those years, she has tutored their writing and taught drama and co-wrote and produced, "The We Nobody Knows," for CrownPlayers. She has served on the 21st Century Collaborative for children and youth. Francine has recently turned her story, "Code47 to BREV Force," into a trilogy. She has also written a manual,for the "Look Good . . . Feel Better" cancer program.

OTHER BOOKS AVAILABLE
Through Golden Quill Press

Code 47 to BREV Force By F. Barish-Stern

HOW TO WRITE YOUR BOOK From an Idea to YourPublished Story By Bobbi R.Madry & F. Barish-Stern

Love Makes the Difference—Reflections on Life in Rockland County By Mary C. Bianchini and Bobbi R. Madry

TELL OTHERS BY Marjorie Struck

Passport to Power By William Thourlby

You Are What You Wear By William Thourlby

There Is Hope By Debby Paine

Sweet Mercy By Rebecca H. Cofer

Mae Sings About Short Vowels By Karen A. Coleman

In His Hands By Fran Toepfer

Challenging Messages From Beyond By Marjorie Struck

Compassion's Lure By Kathleen Lukens

New Horizons-By Francine Cefola and Bobbi Madry

the Grandpa Spider Stories by grandpa spider

The Poem Book By Daniel Windheim and Marjorie Windheim

Opening The Door To A Brighter Future By Daniel Windheim

TO ORDER ADDITIONAL COPIES
TELL IT TO THE FUTURE
Have I Got A Story For You . . .
about the Twentieth Century

Please send _____ book(s) to:

Name _____

Address _____

_____

City _____ State _____ Zip _____

Phone: HOME ( ) _____

WORK ( ) _____

Price per book: $16.95 x _____ $ _____

Virginia residents please add sales tax $ _____

Shipping and handling $ _____
Please add $3.50 for the first book , .50 for each
additional book

TOTAL $ _____

Make check or money order payable to:
Golden Quill Press
PO Box 83
Troutville VA 24175

or visit our website - www.goldenquillpress.com
e-mail info@goldenquillpress.com
Tell Us What is Your Favorite Decade
and Why!

www.ingramcontent.com/pod-product-compliance
Lightning Source LLC
Chambersburg PA
CBHW050637300426
44112CB00012B/1839